WELFARE,
PROPERTY
RIGHTS and
ECONOMIC
POLICY

Essays and Tributes
in Honour of
H. SCOTT GORDON

EDITED BY

Thomas K. Rymes

WELFARE, PROPERTY RIGHTS and ECONOMIC POLICY

Essays and Tributes
in Honour of
H. SCOTT GORDON

EDITED BY

Thomas K. Rymes

Carleton University Press
Ottawa, Canada
1991

ISBN   0-88629-142-9 (paperback)
ISBN   0-88629-143-7 (casebound)

Printed and bound in Canada

Carleton General List

Canadian Cataloguing in Publication Data
Main entry under title:
Welfare, property rights and economic policy :
essays and tributes in honour of H. Scott Gordon

ISBN 0-88629-143-7 (bound)
ISBN 0-88629-142-9 (pbk.)

1. Economic policy. 2. Right of property.
3. Welfare economics. 4. Gordon, H. Scott (Howard
Scott), 1924-   . I. Rymes, T.K. (Thomas Kenneth),
1932-   . II. Gordon, H. Scott (Howard Scott), 1924-.

HB34.W34 1991   338.9   C91-090044-2

Distributed by Oxford University Press Canada,
                70 Wynford Drive,
                Don Mills, Ontario,
                Canada. M3C 1J9
                (416) 441-2941

Cover design: Aerographics Ottawa

Acknowledgments

Carleton University Press gratefully acknowledges the support extended
to its publishing programme by the Canada Council and the Ontario Arts
Council.

H. Scott Gordon 1988
Distinguished Professor of Economics
and Professor of History and Philosophy of Science.
(Indiana News Bureau Photo)

TABLE OF CONTENTS

ACKNOWLEDGMENTS ix
    Thomas K. Rymes, Carleton University

INTRODUCTION 1

Chapter 1
    SCOTT GORDON: AN APPRECIATION
    George W. Wilson, Indiana University 5

Chapter 2
    THE WELFARE IMPLICATIONS OF
    INTERNATIONAL INTERGOVERNMENTAL
    COOPERATION
    Albert Breton, University of Toronto 11

    Comments: **Edwin West,** Carleton University 31
                Dan Usher, Queen's University 36

Chapter 3
    ORIGINS OF THEORIES OF ORGANIZATION:
    THE COMMON PROPERTY ROOT
    Keith Acheson and
    Stephen Ferris, Carleton University 39

    Comments: **André Plourde,** University of Ottawa.................. 65
                M.C. Urquhart, Queen's University 70
                Douglas W. Allen, Simon Fraser University 78
    "A Fish Out of Water: A Fallacy in the
                Application of Common Property"

Chapter 4
    LUNCHEON REMARKS
    David Farr, Carleton University 87
    Stephen Kaliski, Queen's University....................................... 92

Chapter 5
  KEYNESIAN POLICY ANALYSIS, RATIONAL
  EXPECTATIONS, AND THE BANK OF CANADA
  Peter Howitt, University of Western Ontario 95

  Comments: **David Longworth**, Bank of Canada 119
  Nicholas Rowe, Carleton University 126
  "Rules Restored"

Chapter 6
  THE CASE FOR A DISCRETIONARY, POLITICALLY
  RESPONSIBLE CENTRAL BANK
  Thomas K. Rymes, Carleton University 133

  Comments: **Marc Lavoie**, University of Ottawa 155

Chapter 7
  DINNER REMARKS
  Paul Fox, University of Toronto 167

  Ted English, Carleton University 171

  Larry Read, Carleton University 174

PUBLICATIONS OF H. SCOTT GORDON 177

ACKNOWLEDGMENTS

The editor wishes to thank the Social Sciences and Humanities Research Council of Canada for a generous grant to hold the Celebration in honour of H. Scott Gordon, the President of Carleton University for his support, the many friends and participants of the Celebration for their contributions and help, and financial assistance towards publication of this volume from the Dean of Social Sciences, Chair of the Department of Economics, and the Institute of Canadian Studies at Carleton University. With respect to financial help for this volume, special and grateful thanks are due to Principal David Smith and Professor Douglas Purvis, Chairman, Department of Economics at Queen's University and Dean Morton Lowengrub, College of Arts and Sciences, Indiana University for their outstanding generosity.

He is also grateful to Professor George Wilson, School of Business and Dean Morton Lowengrub, of the College of Arts and Sciences, Indiana University for permission to reprint Professor Wilson's appreciation for Scott Gordon from Indiana University, Department of Economics, Alumni Newsletter *The Trend Line* (Fall 1989).

Finally, he wishes to thank Ashish Lall for his assistance during the Celebration and Edie Landau for all her help in making the day a success.

BK Title:

INTRODUCTION

In 1948, H. Scott Gordon joined Carleton University, then six years old, to found officially the Department of Economics. With the almost immediate addition of Ted English, Tom Brewis and Steve Kaliski, the Department immediately grew to one of distinction. In its fortieth year, the Department, now composed of more than 30 members, recognized its founding father by holding a Celebration in his honour on October 12, 1988.

This book contains four essays, together with a number of comments written to celebrate and revere Scott Gordon. It contains as well a selection of appreciative reminiscences of Scott by his friends and colleagues. The papers, comments and reminiscences capture much of the spirit of Scott Gordon. During the day of Celebration, the former President of Carleton, Dr. William Beckel and the Chair of the Department, Professor Ehsan Choudhri, spoke of Professor Gordon's tremendous contribution to the early life and later times of Carleton University, from its early days in the Ladies' College building in downtown Ottawa to those years when Carleton moved to its present beautiful site, near Dow's Lake between the Rideau River and the Rideau Canal, to when it developed into a front rank institution of higher learning with particular strength at the graduate level in the Social Sciences. Scott Gordon played an important and forceful role in building the Department, the Faculty of Social Sciences and Carleton University. Under his care and leadership, the Department of Economics developed a strong sense of independent scholarship which is its healthy trademark today. Carleton's economists represent many schools of thought and approaches to economics. Scott Gordon himself had a catholicity of interests and a natural opposition to the authoritarianism of the orthodox. He was and is an active scholar in many areas of economics: theories of welfare and constitutional form and property rights, monetary policy and the history of economic, political and social thought. No closeted scholar, he has been very active in public debate in Canada.

Scott Gordon left Carleton in 1966 and continued his distinguished career at Indiana University, and, for many summers since 1970, at Queen's University where he has offered for senior undergraduate and graduate students his renowned course on the history of economic thought.

Professor Mac Urquhart kindly informed me that Scott was a member of the first summer group in 1953 that joined the Institute for Economic Research at Queen's University. It was there that he finished his famous paper "The Economic Theory of a Common Property Resource: The Fishery," (*Journal of Political Economy*, 1954).

In the morning of the Celebration Day, Professor Albert Breton presented his paper "The Welfare Implications of International Intergovernmental Co-Operation" which provoked much discussion led by the comments by Professors Dan Usher and Edwin West. Before lunch, Professors Keith Acheson and Steve Ferris, in celebration of Scott's seminal work on property rights, presented their appreciation "Origins of Theories of Organization: The Common Property Root," accompanied by comments from André Plourde and Mac Urquhart. This session stimulated remarks by Doug Allen, "A Fish Out of Water: a Fallacy in the Application of Common Property" which is included in this volume, as one indication of how Scott Gordon's original work in the common property fisheries problem continues to stimulate fruitful thought and discussion.

Lunch in the Senate Lounge was enlivened by remarks by David Farr, now retired from the Department of History at Carleton but who, along with Scott, was one of Carleton's originals; Don Rowat, from Carleton's Political Science Department and Scott's former Carleton colleague, Steve Kaliski, now also at Queen's.

In the afternoon two papers were presented in appreciation of Scott Gordon's work on monetary economics. Peter Howitt in his "Keynesian Policy Analysis, Rational Expectations, and the Bank of Canada," argued that, in the light of rational expectations analysis, Keynesian policy analysis and a positive role for monetary policy remains valid. Tom Rymes argued that, in a world of "supernonneutrality" where central banks would appear to be so many fifth wheels, there remains a case for a discretionary, democratically-responsible central bank. A lively discussion led by David Longworth, George Freeman, Nicholas Rowe and Marc Lavoie ensued.

A dinner was held that evening in Scott and Barbara's honour in Carleton University's Faculty Club. Remarks were recorded by Scott's Carleton colleagues, Ted English and Larry Read; and by Paul Fox from Toronto all with whom Scott collaborated in published work.

Letters and telegrams of congratulations and best wishes were read from Scott's colleagues and friends from all across Canada and the U.S.A. In particular, he was saluted by the Dean and Faculty of the College of Arts and Sciences at Indiana University where he has been since leaving Carleton.

The day was marked by the warmth, the scholarship and the great academic friendship which has so characterized Scott Gordon's life. A distinguished scholar, past president of the Canadian Economics Association, a member of the Royal Society of Canada, Scott Gordon is the founding father of Carleton University's Department of Economics. We are very proud of him.

T.K. Rymes
December 1990

Chapter I

SCOTT GORDON: AN APPRECIATION

George W. Wilson, Indiana University

Scott Gordon retired on June 30, 1989 after 23 years at Indiana University and a distinguished career as teacher and scholar dating back to 1948. He was born in Halifax, Nova Scotia, in 1924, and attended public school, high school, and college there, obtaining his college degree from Dalhousie University in 1944. A scholarship led him to New York and Columbia University for the AM degree, followed by a fellowship at McGill University, Montreal, and a year as lecturer in economics.

I first met H.S.G. (the H stands for Howard, a name he abhors so much that he often signs his publications by dropping it altogether, even the initial) in 1948 when I was a student at Carleton University (then Carleton College) in Ottawa. Carleton was a new institution created shortly after World War II to meet a perceived need for non-sectarian higher education in Canada's capital. Being new, it sought to obtain the brightest young faculty it could muster. Scott was one of the vanguard of this remarkable group, who turned out to be truly outstanding intellectuals in a wide variety of fields. Because of their success, Carleton University has now become a large, important, and influential part of higher learning in Canada.

Scott was an important part of this development. He organized the economics department at Carleton in 1948 and was its chairman for the next six years. He participated in many other ways in the achievements of Carleton during these critical formative years and rose to the rank of full professor in 1957. He was such an integral part of the school that his colleagues and successors at Carleton honoured him with a *festschrift* in 1988, some 25 years after his departure for Indiana University, on which this volume reports.

During his Carleton period he also embarked upon a high-level research career. A summer job at the Department of Fisheries in Ottawa led to his well-known article "The Economic Theory of a Common

Property Resource: The Fishery" (*Journal of Political Economy*, 1954), which became the basis of virtually a new field in which scholarship continues to the present. It is probably his most influential work.

A visit to Cambridge University, England, in 1954-55 on a Social Science Research Council of Canada fellowship resulted in one of his most fascinating articles, "The London *Economist* and the High Tide of Laissez-Faire," a lead article in the 1955 *Journal of Political Economy*. This little gem almost never saw the light of day. Upon showing the manuscript to Piero Sraffa at Cambridge and asking where it should be sent for publication, Sraffa replied, "Why publish it? You've had your fun!" So much for publish or perish at Cambridge!

This highly successful early output, which also included other papers, was followed by his involvement in a major economic "scandal" in Canada. A recession occurred in the late 1950s, leading to very high rates of unemployment. However, the Governor of the Bank of Canada persisted in policies designed to prevent the federal government from running a deficit large enough to alleviate the situation. Indeed, with unemployment rates over 9 percent during the first quarter of 1959 and over 10 percent in 1961, the Bank of Canada pursued a tight money policy to combat a nonexistent inflation! As an unrepentant and outraged Keynesian, Scott led a group of economists in drafting a scathing attack that appeared in a widely distributed pamphlet entitled *The Economists Versus the Bank of Canada* (1961). He himself penned several other more scholarly articles dealing with irrational monetary policies and other related matters. The Bank of Canada critique became a minor *cause célèbre* at the time, and Scott was at the centre of it.

Shortly after this, he and I joined in preparing a study that appeared in 1965, concerning Canada's need and resources for the Twentieth Century Fund. Amongst other contributions to the volume, he wrote a marvellous introductory chapter capturing the essence of the Canadian experience — a minor classic of its kind. Prior to this collaboration, we had remained in touch since my graduation from Carleton in 1950 — in part because he wanted to make sure his students from only the second graduating class were performing respectably, but mostly because we got along well.

It was during our frequent contacts over the Canadian book that he broached the possibility of leaving Carleton for a larger university and inquired about Indiana University. I was shocked and flattered — shocked because few of us who graduated from Carleton could visualize it without Scott Gordon, and flattered to think that my favourite professor might want to come to a place that had accepted me!

Unforeseen but strangely related events pushed me into the chairmanship of Indiana University's Department of Economics. My first phone call from the office in Ballantine Hall was to offer Scott Gordon a job, which he accepted immediately saying "I was just waiting to be asked." I should emphasize that this seemingly casual hiring would now be grounds for dismissal, or worse, of the chairman. There was no search committee. I neither told nor consulted anyone in advance, and indeed did not even have a position available. Those were the days when even administration was sometimes fun.

In any event, a position was "given" by a somewhat irate dean. Scott and family arrived that fall, 1966, and quickly confirmed my highest hopes and expectations. I did however have some qualms about Carleton's losing him. In fact, some years later at a conference in Montreal, then-Prime Minister of Canada Lester Pearson, noting that I was from Indiana University, assailed me with, "So you're the one who stole Scott Gordon from Canada!" I felt only marginal guilt.

Scott's tenure at Indiana has been a huge success. His research proliferated mainly along the lines of his lifelong passion for the history of economic thought, which he taught so brilliantly, and broadened to the more general and difficult field of the history and meaning of ideas. He wrote about Marx and *Das Kapital*, Bagehot, Keynes, John Stuart Mill, Edgeworth, Marshall, Malthus, Frank Night, John Rawls, and even John Kenneth Galbraith. His article on the "Close of the Galbraithian System" (*Journal of Political Economics*, 1968) angered that Harvard gentleman into a response revealing that he had received royalties from certain publications that Scott believed were of dubious merit. The other authors noted above were treated more seriously. At least they never responded in anger.

By the early 1970s Scott began to move more into social science, philosophy, and even sociobiology, although never forgetting the mother science, economics. He published his first major book, *Welfare, Justice, and Freedom,* in 1980. It received excellent reviews and illustrated the breadth as well as the depth of his thinking. His work is readable and understandable, unlike so much of the jargon-laden material often associated with discussions of such esoteric concepts. One does not need to agree with Scott Gordon on all points to be impressed with his incredible grasp and knowledge of so many areas. For example, I don't agree with him on various points in Marx, Keynes, and Marshall, but he sure has Galbraith's number — and goat, too.

More recently, in fact for the past four or five years, he has been working on what is bound to become a *magnum opus* or even a *summa*! It is not yet published, but a contract has been signed. Entitled "The Proper Study of Mankind: An Introduction to the History and Philosophy of Social Sciences," it is the biggest single enterprise he has ever attempted. The first part is an advanced treatise on the history of economic thought, followed by similar analyses of sociological and political thought as well as historiography and others. It is a real *tour de force*. Adding to this and following up many provocative openings will keep him glued to his word processor for decades to come.

But Scott's tenure at Indiana University has not been confined merely to research and publication. Publication stems, in his case, from a perceptive, inquiring, and energetic mind. This makes him a wonderful conversationalist. People also seek him out for advice and counsel, which he invariably gives with much concern and wisdom. His voice was always eagerly awaited, for example, in the Bloomington Faculty Council, to which he was often elected. As further evidence of the high regard in which his colleagues hold him, in 1981 he was made distinguished professor of economics on the unanimous recommendation of an all-faculty committee, and in 1983 he was invited to become a member of the Department of History and Philosophy of Science.

He regularly teaches courses of HPS, some of which he personally has designed, and is involved in doctoral programs, recruiting, and curricular matters there as well as in economics. In both departments he is a popular teacher despite his high standards. After one of his classes at Carleton he advised that while I wrote an "A paper," nobody knew enough about the subject matter, including himself, to warrant an A, so he gave me a B. I'm told this doesn't happen any more.

His ability as a teacher and scholar is widely known. Many years ago Queen's University in Kingston, Ontario, sought to lure him away from Indiana University but had to settle for his services only from June to August each year. Indiana University had him from September to May. In this way he assuaged his Canadian conscience.

Scott Gordon is everyman's version of an intellectual, a professor's professor so to speak, but without the dullness and pretence that such visions often conjure up. He has a good sense of humour, laughs a lot, tells a good story, and on occasion has a certain pixie-ish quality. In a published volume of four public lectures he once gave under the pretentious title of *Social Science and Modern Man* (1970), he arranged the wording over two pages, dealing, I think, with some of the lunacies of Marshall McCluhan, so that the heavily italicized capital letters at the start of each sentence spelled out an obscenity precisely describing the excrement of male cattle.

Though Scott has retired, he will be around Bloomington writing, conversing, advising, giving the occasional lecture, flitting off to England and Italy with his wife and friends, enjoying music and opera. In short, not much will change. Scholarship and camaraderie are his life. The phrase "Great Scott" is more than an exclamation. It is descriptive of one of Indiana University's most impressive professors.

JEL
H77
F13   F02

Chapter II

THE WELFARE IMPLICATIONS OF INTERNATIONAL INTERGOVERNMENTAL COOPERATION

Albert Breton, University of Toronto

1. INTRODUCTION

The literature on international co-operation often poses the question of the desirability of co-operation in the following terms: the government of a country wishes to implement a policy of fiscal expansion which it deems will benefit its citizens. Because that action will worsen its balance of trade, it chooses not to expand. If, however, that government could co-ordinate its decision with those of its trading partners and all adopted an expansionary fiscal stance, each one's trade balance would remain closer to balance. Thus by co-operating, all countries could pursue policies which are better for each one of them, a situation that is not possible if each is acting alone. Stating the matter in this way may be said to point to the benefits of co-operation. But, as many critics have noted, there are costs to co-operation, among which is the possibility of collusion.

There are other benefits in posing the problem of international co-operation in the way I have just described. For one thing, it forces analysts to address immediately problems of macroeconomics, exchange rate, trade, debt and other similar concrete policy co-operation issues. But there are also other costs. These mostly derive from a propensity on the part of analysts to take international institutions for granted and to assume that these are almost incidental to the well-functioning of the world order. In other words, posing the problem of intergovernmental co-operation in the concrete and immediate terms of day-to-day policy issues presupposes that intergovernmental relations are, in the absence of institutions, stable relations.

Given the great interest in and the considerable pressure for reform in the *modus operandi* of intergovernmental co-operation, it is important to analyse all aspects of this problem and, therefore, to also examine what, for lack of a better word, might be called the fundamentals of the matter. I will begin, in the next section, by arguing that intergovernmental relations in the world order are competitive relations just as they are in federal systems [see Breton (1985)]. This done, I will, in Section 3, argue that these competitive relations tend to be unstable. In Sections 4 and 5 I will, in turn, describe how the problem of stability is institutionally addressed in federal systems and in the international order. I will underline the "inferiority" of international compared to federalist institutions. Finally, in Section 6, I will indicate what basic problems intergovernmental co-operation at the international level must resolve in the light of how federalist stability is achieved.

2. Intergovernmental Competition

Governments are not monoliths. They are conglomerations of numerous centres of power — branches and quasi-autonomous bodies — which compete with each other. However, for the purpose of the discussion that follows, I will treat central or national governments in every country as unitary entities. I will also assume that there are imperatives of one kind or another which turn these governments toward the preferences and interests of citizens. Electoral competition, as a force leading to such a result, may not be consistent with the assumption of unitary monolithic bodies, but if it is not, one could assume that the obligation to economize on resources allocated to the maintenance of public order could generate the same result. However that may be, I need the assumption of unitary governments only to simplify the presentation.

More substantially, I assume that these governments compete with each other. Before asking how, let me enquire into why they do this. In conventional or textbook theory, governments compete with each other either to attract or to repel citizens who are "voting with their feet" or more precisely shopping around for the most appropriate local public goods and tax schedules. This Tiebout (1956) mechanism has even become entrenched in public finance discussions of federalism. It is true that the assumption is sometimes camouflaged by the device of assuming "competing communities" — not competing governments, but if citizens are really shopping around, it is easy to assume that "agencies," which we can call governments, will perceive the possibility of garnering net benefits by catering to the wants of citizens and so will be competing with each other.

Some international migration is surely of the same type as the one Tiebout and his followers have postulated to characterize community migration. That is even more obvious if one includes in the output of governments, not only policies such as national defence, environmental protection, income redistribution and education, but also religious persecution, censorship and racial discrimination which have to be counted if public output is to be correctly defined. However, even if it exists, an international Tiebout mechanism is surely much too weak a reed on which to peg the assumption of international intergovernmental competition.

But there is an alternative to Tiebout. In two provoking papers, Salmon (1987a and 1987b) has shown that if the citizens of a jurisdiction can use the performance of the government of another jurisdiction as a benchmark to evaluate what their own government is doing, they will give or withhold support from the latter on the basis of that rating. If electoral competition is allowed, the process will intensify that competition and if it is not, it will raise the cost of maintaining public order. In either case, the end result will be that governments will be competing with each other.

The Salmon mechanism obviously requires that information about the behaviour of other governments be available to citizens. If such information is sparse the mechanism will be weak. No body of evidence is available that would allow us to evaluate the strength of the mechanism, but the existence of bamboo and iron curtains, press censorship and other similar phenomena is evidence that the mechanism exists and has some strength. It is interesting that the Salmon mechanism requires a failure of Tiebout dynamics. Indeed, in Tiebout models, equilibrium is achieved when the population is partitioned in such a way that all communities are homogeneous. The Salmon mechanism, on the contrary, requires that in the benchmark community there be people with the same preferences as those, in another community, making the comparison. I note finally that if the Salmon mechanism is powerful enough, it can explain the tax and benefit capitalization into housing price, which Oates (1969) first diagnosed, without appealing to mobility between communities.

There is, furthermore, an enormous amount of evidence which can be given a rationale by reference to a Salmon mechanism. The evidence pertains to the relationship of governments in federal states, not to the relationship of governments in the world order. However, I will point to some facts that indicate that if the same studies were done at the international level, similar results to those obtained for federations, would be obtained.

The available evidence pertains to the rate of diffusion of policies over jurisdictions. I have reviewed that literature elsewhere (Breton, 1988), and, as a consequence, will be very brief. The observed pattern of diffusion is as follows: a jurisdiction adopts a particular policy; in time a few others do the same, but eventually the number of adopters increases rapidly to taper off sometimes close to saturation, sometimes not. The pattern describes an ogive or S-curve. To my knowledge, Walker (1969) was the first to explain the pattern of diffusion of the 88 policies he analysed by reference to competition. More recently Reinganum (1983) and especially Romano (1985) have underlined that connection. That intergovernmental competition based on a Salmon mechanism provides a rationale for the pattern of policy diffusion is easily understood within Schumpeter's (1911, 1942) model of development which assumes that innovations are introduced in the economy by the entrepreneurs and are then taken up by those we may conveniently call "corporate managers" on the basis of mundane cost-benefit calculations. The innovator-follower process generates a cycle not unlike an ogive curve [see Shumpeter, but also Samuelson (1982)].

Many of the researchers who have estimated S-curves have stressed that the exact shape of any of these curves will depend on information flows. If we assume that the volume of available information increases as the number of jurisdictions adopting a particular policy increases, the ogive would take the shape of the familiar logistic curve. The evidence is consistent with the notion that the S-curves, generated by Salmon-Schumpeter processes, are logistic curves.

As evidence that competition works in the same way at the international level, let me point to the phenomenon of privatization and deregulation which some observers find difficult to understand [see, for example, Kay and Thompson (1986)]. The difficulty is that the phenomenon which began a decade or so ago has been gaining momentum. The policy has, indeed, been and is being adopted by right-of-centre and by left-of-centre governments, by governments of developed and of less developed countries and by democratic and non-democratic governments. Given this fact, ideology, which was advanced as an explanation of the phenomenon — and may have played a role in the early stages of diffusion — is powerless to rationalize its subsequent evolution. The need for funds to cover current budget deficits can surely not explain deregulation which yields no revenues. Other explanations based on a realignment of interest groups or on the internal contradictions of the welfare state simply do not explain why the phenomenon is essentially worldwide, because countries are too different for these explanations to hold.

But the diffusion of privatization and deregulation poses no problem in a model of intergovernmental competition on Salmon-Schumpeter lines. Indeed, if we assume that the policy raises the private yield on capital — as theory tells us it must — then countries which do not follow the leaders would simply lose capital, as do the firms that lag behind in the Schumpeterian model of development.

I have so far referred to the policies of government, except for privatization and deregulation, in very abstract terms. For the sake of concreteness, let me mention that historically governments have competed internationally for physical capital, market shares, high technology, human capital, not to mention land, natural resources and reputation. They compete for these things by implementing an array of policies which are too well known to require documentation.

3. The Stability of Competition

We must distinguish between two different sources of instability. One is essentially technical and results from (say) non-convexities of production technologies. These may be either "inherent" as when increasing returns produce "natural" monopolies or may be derivative as when strong negative externalities transform a convex into a non-convex production set [see Baumol (1964) and Baumol and Bradford (1972)]. Instability may also result from adjustment coefficients which are either too large or too small leading to cumulative movements in a particular direction as happens in certain models of population mobility [see Stiglitz (1977)] and in many models of macroeconomic growth. Cycling in majority voting and in logrolling models are other examples of technical instability.

The second source of instability is institutional. We are now discovering that technical instability can be prevented by institutional arrangements. That literature is too voluminous to be summarized here; I therefore, simply illustrate. Alchian and Demsetz (1972) have suggested an alternative rationale to that of Coase (1937) for the existence of firms. In their model, firms are institutions designed to deal with shirking or free riding — surely an important source of instability. Becker and Stigler (1974) have argued that the posting of bonds as a way of preventing malfeasant behaviour, while Klein and Leffler (1981) and Shapiro (1983) have shown that reputation will prevent quality deterioration in competitive contests. Leland (1979) has made the point that licensing is a possible institutional device for dealing with the instability resulting from asymmetric information. Williamson (1983) has argued that credible commitments can permit exchanges in contexts in which they would otherwise vanish. Mathewson and Winter (1985) have demonstrated that franchising is an efficient institutional arrangement to deal with one type of instability inherent in the "agency problem." As a last example, I mention Shepsle and Weingast's (1981) model of agenda control as a solution to the instability of logrolling.

It is difficult to exaggerate the value of this research. It should not bring us to conclude, however, that every time that technical instability rears its head, institutional arrangements automatically arise to deal with it. Institutional instability is the situation that arises when institutions do not appear to deal with technical instability or when the institutions that do appear are flawed in some significant way. It is, as a consequence, very difficult to observe institutional instability. Still its existence can be documented.

In Section 5, I will argue that some stability of intergovernmental competition at the international level can be achieved by an effective hegemonic power. If such a power exists and if it takes its responsibilities seriously, competition can be nearly stable. If this argument is correct, one would have to conclude that in the absence of an hegemonic power, international relations would be unstable. At the end of World War I the United Kingdom, which had been the world's hegemonic power for a century, was unable to continue performing that role and the United States was unwilling to assume it. For nearly 25 years, there was then no effective hegemonic power in the world.

There is debate about the evidence — there always is. But it is hard to read Nurkse's (1944) and Kindleberger's (1986) analytical narratives of the events of those years — repeated exchange rate devaluations, tariff wars and other beggar-my-neighbour actions — without concluding that the world order was very unstable. Indeed, the instability appears to have been so pervasive that the period provides as close a laboratory experiment as we are likely to have in the social sciences of a world without stabilizing institutions.

Let me point to another piece of evidence, though not one pertaining to international relations. In a paper which has not only provoked an enormous debate, but which has also had considerable influence, Carey

(1974) has argued that intergovernmental competition for revenues produced by the supply of corporate charters has led state governments in the United States to make corporate statutes increasingly more appealing to managers — to those who "buy" the incorporation and re-incorporation charters — by increasing their freedom vis-à-vis stockholders. Carey describes the process as a "movement toward the least common denominator" (p. 663), as a "race for the bottom" (p. 666), and as an "application of Gresham's law" (p. 698), all expressions which describe instability.

Carey's paper was not long without a response. But though his argument had been about "fiduciary responsibility and fairness" and about "shareholder's rights," his critics [for example, Winter (1977)], Fischel (1982) and Romano (1985)] focused on the earnings performance of corporations that changed their charter domicile to Delaware. Again the evidence is hard to interpret. However, the fact that Carey's paper provoked a judicial response [in Singer v. Manafox Co. 380A, 2d 969 (1977)], would seem to indicate that he had a point. For the purpose of deciding on the stability of intergovernmental competition, this case may be less clear cut than the one pertaining to international relations during the interwar years, but, it seems to me, still indicates a tendency toward instability.

The only other evidence I will mention pertains to the "urban crisis" in the United States. There is agreement that the crisis results from a movement of the population from the urban centres to the suburbs. Bird and Slack (1983), who contrasted the state of cities in Canada and the U.S., concluded that the situation is better in Canada because of larger grants from the province to the municipal governments and because of a more centralized assignment of powers in Canada than in the U.S.[1] The upshot of these propositions is that there is excessive or destabilizing local mobility in the U.S. which does not happen in Canada because the institutional context is different.

I conclude from the above that in the absence of certain institutional arrangements — to which I immediately turn my attention — intergovernmental competition tends to be unstable. Another way of making the same point, but from a different perspective, is to say that in an institution-less state of nature, property rights that would insure that the competition between governments would be stable do not exist and so competition is unstable.

4. FEDERALIST STABILITY

One of the most important dimensions of federalism is intergovernmental competition. In some instances, that competition has led to the demise of federations [see Riker and Lemco (1987)]. But in the majority of federal states, intergovernmental competition is not unstable. What is it that insures stability? I have argued elsewhere (Breton, 1988) that stability is guaranteed by a third party and that that third party is the central government. I do not repeat this argument here, but assume that this is the case.

It is obviously not the simple existence of a central authority that produces stability — confederal states have central authorities, but have typically been unstable. For the central government to be able to stabilize competition, certain conditions must be satisfied. Two are so basic that they are often overlooked in discussions of the matter. The first of these is that the federal government should be answerable to the citizenry at large and not to member governments. In democratic states, this means that politicians at the federal level should be elected by the citizens of the whole country and not be appointed by provincial politicians. It is clear why this is necessary: in case of conflict, provincial politicians cannot have the power to terminate appointments and prevent the solution of problems.

The second condition is just as important. The federal government must have the power to levy taxes directly from the people. Again, it cannot rely for its revenues on transfers from the member units and for the same reason that requires direct elections. The Fathers of the American Constitution, meeting in Philadelphia in 1787, have been justly credited as being the inventors of federalism. The invention lies in the formulation and implementation of the foregoing two conditions.

These, however, are not sufficient to guarantee stability. Another is an entrenched division of constitutional powers that gives the federal government the capacity to block or prevent the implementation of beggar-my-neighbour policies by member units. By entrenched I mean a division of powers that cannot be altered unilaterally by one level of government. One way of dealing with competitive instability is to centralize powers. That was the solution suggested by the Rowel-Sirois Royal Commission on Dominion-Provincial Relations (1940) which had diagnosed instability in intergovernmental competition in the Canadian federation of the 1930s. However, centralization solves the problem by suppressing the reality: it is cure by death. Entrenchment prevents that type of cure.

But in addition to being entrenched, the division of powers must make it possible for the federal government to intervene if a province tries to export its tax burdens to other provinces, to impose tariffs or other impediments to the movement of goods and services between provinces or to adopt other policies of that kind. It must be able to do so not because these policies are "inefficient" from an economic point of view — which will be the case if costs exceed benefits — but because these policies can, if unchecked, lead to cumulative destabilizing responses and counter-responses. The federal government's role, in other words, is not to stop a provincial government from inflicting net costs on its citizens — that is the responsibility of the provincial citizens themselves — but to prevent destabilizing responses from neighbouring jurisdictions.

It is still possible, with the three above conditions satisfied, for inter-governmental competition to be unstable. That will be especially the case if there is a great disparity in the size, wealth and power of member units. In Canada, Prince Edward Island is less than one-fifth of one percent the size of Ontario and in the United States Delaware is even smaller relative to California. In the competition for human and physical capital, for head offices, for research laboratories and for a host of other things, smaller provinces are likely to be systematic losers. If they were allowed to go bankrupt and disappear that would create no stability problem, but since for a number of reasons bankruptcy is not a real possibility, a problem exists.[2]

There are two different types of policies that can be implemented to deal with this problem: intergovernmental grants and regional policies. Because they are substitutes one for the other, though not necessarily perfect substitutes, one or both policies may be used, depending on the severity of the problem. Regional policies may be camouflaged as defence expenditures, as is current practice in the U.S., but they can obviously be overt as they have been in federal states for over two centuries. Interjurisdictional grants and regional policies as instruments to stabilize competition are, therefore, "allocational" policies, though they will obviously have redistributional consequences.

Riker and Menco (1987) in their empirical study of 40 federations — past and present — were able to establish that the greater the variance in the size of member units, the more unstable the federation. If, in addition, we assume that stability increases as the number of units grows, we would expect, if intergovernmental grants and regional policies are primarily stabilization devices, that their incidence will be less in federations with a large number of constituent units which are more or less of equal size. Casual observations would seem to corroborate that expectation.

Stable intergovernmental competition in federal states results from a number of institutional arrangements. These all contribute in one way or the other, depending on the nature of the problem, to guarantee that competition is stable and potentially productive. Institutions are generally susceptible to improvement, but genuine improvement requires that we understand why these institutions exist in the first place.

5. HEGEMONIC STABILITY

In a masterful synthesis and extension of available propositions, models and evidence, Keohane (1984) has forcefully argued that intergovernmental competition in the world order cannot be stable unless a hegemonic power initially assumes the responsibility for that stability. Keohane goes on to argue that once the institutions that produce stability are in place, the demise of the hegemon need not cause instability, because member governments will understand the benefits they derive from these institutions — which in the literature on hegemonic stability are called regimes. It is unfortunate, I believe, that the literature on hegemonic stability never looks into the causes of federalist stability. It is true, of course, that the two worlds of research and enquiry never intersect. Furthermore, international relations scholars confront virtually nothing else except competitive instability, while federalism scholars study a world of stability.[3] It is still interesting and instructive, however, to contrast the two.

When we do so, we are immediately struck by the fact that the four conditions that I discussed in the previous section as necessary for the stability of intergovernmental competition are only very poorly satisfied in the international as compared to federalist contexts. To see this, let me follow Keohane and distinguish between two possible phases of organization: one where there is an effective hegemon and another when only the regimes that the hegemon has either created or supported survive.

A hegemonic power — the United States government in the present era or the government of the United Kingdom during the 19th century — is, like the central government of a federation, a third party which, if it is a truly effective hegemon, can assume the responsibility for stabilizing competition. But, as I noted earlier, existence is not enough — certain conditions must also be satisfied. Let me look at the four discussed in the last section in turn.

The governing politicians in the hegemon are clearly not elected by all those who fall within its sphere of influence. Indeed, only the hegemonic power's citizens are allowed to vote for its governing politicians. Because diplomacy — the representation of the periphery's interests at the centre — is a poor substitute for electoral representation, the hegemon will be led, the stronger the degree of competition, to propose and support the creation and development of international institutions — regimes — in which the interests of the periphery will somehow be debated, and, hopefully, influence the design of the hegemon's international policies. Effective regimes remain, however, imperfect substitutes for elected assemblies.

Hegemonic powers do not have the power to tax outside their own frontier. But third parties need resources — sometimes a large volume of resources — to stabilize intergovernmental competition. Though, as far as I am aware, the phenomenon is largely unstudied, it seems that a large part of the resources available to the hegemon for stabilizing competition come from taxing its own citizens. This can take any number of forms: the hegemon may carry the bulk of the costs of common undertakings such as defence, it may make resources available to cover balance of payments deficits such as happened with the Marshall Plan, it may carry a disproportionate fraction of the cost of maintaining international bodies, etc.

The hegemon will, of course, also try, often indirectly, to obtain resources from those countries that are within its sphere of influence. It may, for example, provide the "key" currency and collect seigniorage. It will, of course, by all the means at its disposal, try to have all countries pay a share of common undertakings and of the operations of regimes. The enormous literature on imperialism and on dependency, well summarized by Mommsen (1977) and by Griffin and Gurley (1985), which must surely be pointing to some real phenomenon of the world of international relations indicates that hegemons also use their power to structure the rules of competition to their benefit, thus indirectly taxing the periphery. There is no need to insist that these various devices are poor substitutes for some constitutional power to tax.

There is no division of powers in the world order. It is obviously recognized that some phenomena transcend national boundaries and could lead to an international division of powers, but, in practice the hegemon is assigned no powers. Referring to theories of federalism, the world order is organized like a confederation and, therefore, tends to have the inherent instability of confederal states.

Finally, there are no formal grants systems and regional development programs in the world order, although hegemons will, again when competition is rife, support institutions such as the World Bank, United Nations Relief and Rehabilitation Agency, and others which are substitutes for the formal policies of federal states. The hegemonic power may itself put in place programs of "foreign aid" which mimic the programs of regional aid in federations.

The withdrawal — partial or complete — of the hegemon, either because it has stopped being an hegemonic power, because it has lost the will to act in that capacity or because it is preoccupied with other matters will lead, according to Keohane, to its replacement by regimes which the hegemon had ealier nurtured. It would be unduly repetitive to review, for regimes, the four conditions that insure stability in federal states. However, a moment's reflection will indicate that regimes can meet these conditions even less satisfactorily than can hegemons. It is at this juncture that the question of intergovernmental co-operation at the international level must be posed.

6. CO-OPERATION

The United States is not the hegemonic power that it was in the quarter century or so following World War II, but it still has the capacity to be a powerful hegemon. The greater preoccupation of recent years with the competition over social and economic systems and the massive reallocation of resources in that direction has, of course, meant that a lower priority was accorded to hegemonic stability in its own sphere of influence. But, given the will, the capacity is still there.

In what is referred to as the Western World, the third party function of stabilizing intergovernmental competition is, therefore, assigned to hegemonic America and to the international regimes that have been developed and maintained over the last 40 years or so. These two sources of stability are not as effective, I have argued in the last section, as the central governments of federal states when they are engaged in the same endeavour.[4] This is why stability of competition requires co-operation.

Co-operation is not an easy phenomenon to discuss, the enormous literature that would appear to suggest the opposite notwithstanding. I do not wish to address the modes of co-operative behaviour. What I would like to stress is what co-operation should achieve. It will come as no surprise that I assign to co-operation at the international level the task of reproducing what the four conditions for stability achieve in federal states.

Co-operation should, therefore, strive to achieve a representation at the centre of the interests of the citizenry of the periphery. This is, obviously, more easily said than done because officials in international regimes are bureaucrats. They are, in other words, appointees. The rule which says that the representatives of the representatives of the people are *not*, themselves, representatives of the people, holds. Still, if co-operation does not get organized to reflect, as best it can, the preferences and interests of people, it degenerates into collusion which is probably worse than some degree of competitive instability.

Condition two pertaining to the power to tax and condition four to the ability of the centre, by expending resources, to insure that smaller units are not systematically penalized, can be discussed together. At this stage in the development of society, the probability that some power to tax will be assigned to a central authority is nil. That is easy to understand especially if the centre is a national hegemon in which citizens of the periphery have no voice. It is the simple consequence of another old rule which asserts that there is no taxation without representation.

Transferring resources to the centre is, then, another task of co-operation. This is not easy to achieve. National governments much prefer to use their foreign aid individually as an instrument of competition, to give their country leverage in trade, investment contracts and other things of that kind. That defeats the whole purpose. A test of true co-operation is the transfer of foreign aid to one or more central bodies in lieu of assigning them the power to tax. If that is done, the capacity of the centre to allocate these funds to effectively stabilize intergovernmental competition will be enhanced. Indeed, if nation states do the allocation themselves on an individual basis, they have no incentive to give any weight to stabilizing competition.

Finally, co-operation will be effective if it achieves an informal division of powers between the centre and the periphery that can be taken to be more or less entrenched. This is most probably the area of greatest difficulty as the events of the last decade indicate. However without something like it, conflicts fester and degenerate. The debate in the economics profession about the desirability of world wide macroeconomic policies is to a degree a debate about the wisdom of reassigning part of the power over fiscal and monetary policy to one or more central institutions. It may well turn out that wisdom will emerge when we discover a median way of doing such a reassignment. Federal countries have often been ingenious in this area. In Canada, for example, judges are appointed by the federal government, but paid by the provinces, thus increasing the independence of the judiciary. Finding ways of dividing powers internationally, through co-operation, is required if we wish stable international relations.

I have argued in the preceding pages that intergovernmental relations are competitive, and that that competition in some institution-less state of nature is unstable. I have also argued that stability can be achieved by developing institutions for that purpose. I have looked at how this is achieved in federal states because the relations of governments in these states mimic those of governments in the international order.

I have then turned my attention to the institutions which produce stability at the international level and argued that they were less effective than those in federal contexts. This led me to suggest that co-operation could, by reproducing the conditions of federalist stability, generate greater stability in the international community, even in the face of a weak hegemon and only moderately effective international regimes.

NOTES

[1] Bird and Slack also mention the comparative youth of Canadian cities and the consequent expansion of tax bases as cities grow.

[2] Those who study the effect of interjurisdictional grants and of other policies of that type usually assume that interjurisdictional mobility is stable [see, for example, Courchene (1970) and Winer and Gauthier (1982)]. Those who analyze "voting with feet" models of local public goods often conclude that that mobility is unstable [see, for example, Stiglitz (1977), Rose-Ackerman (1979) and Westhoff (1979)]. In models of institution-less intergovernmental competition, it is best to make the second assumption.

[3] The enormous, often sentimental and hopeful, literature on "cooperative federalism" is surely the product of an insight — albeit, repressed — that federalist competition is not always stable.

[4] I lack the space to discuss the role of the internal structure of the central government of federal states — what Smiley (1971), Cairns (1979) and Gibbins (1982) among many others have analyzed under the heading of "intrastate federalism" — in fulfilling that role. I have summarized and reinterpreted that literature in Breton (1988).

REFERENCES

A.A. Alchian and H. Demsetz, "Production, Information Costs, and Economic Organization," *American Economic Review*, (Vol. LXII, No. 5, December 1972), pp. 777-795.

W.J. Baumol, "External Economies and Second-Order Optimality Conditions," *American Economic Review*, (Vol. 54, No. 4, Pt. I, June 1964), pp. 358-372.

W.J. Baumol and D.F. Bradford, "Detrimental Externalities and Non-Convexity of the Production Set," *Economica*, (Vol. 39, No. 154, May 1972), pp. 160-176.

G. S. Becker and G.J. Stigler, "Law Enforcement, Malfeasance, and Compensation of Enforcers," *Journal of Legal Studies*, (Vol. 3, No. 1, January 1974), pp. 1-18.

R.M. Bird and N.E. Slack, *Urban Public Finance in Canada*, (Toronto: Butterworths, 1983).

A. Breton, "Supplementary Report," *Report of the Royal Commission on the Economic Union and Development Prospects for Canada*, Volume III, (Ottawa: Supply and Services, 1985), Reprinted as "Towards a Theory of Competitive Federalism," *European Journal of Political Economy*, (Vol. 3, Nos. 1 & 2, 1987), pp. 263-329.

A. Breton, "Intranational Intergovernmental Competition," Typescript, 1988.

A.C. Cairns, *From Interstate to Intrastate Federalism*, (Kingston: Queen's University, Institute of Intergovernmental Relations, 1979).

W.L. Carey, "Federalism and Corporate Law: Reflections Upon Delaware," *Yale Law Journal*, (Vol. 83, No. 4, March 1974), pp. 663-705.

R.H. Coase, "The Nature of the Firm," *Economica*, (Vol. 4, November 1937), pp. 386-405.

T.J. Courchene, "Interprovincial Migration and Economic Adjustment," *Canadian Journal of Economics*, (Vol. 3, No. 4, November 1970), pp. 550-576.

D.R. Fischel, "The 'Race to the Bottom' Revisited: Reflections on Recent Developments in Delaware's Corporation Law," *Northwestern University Law Review*, (Vol. 76, No. 6, 1982), pp. 913-945.

R. Gibbins, *Regionalism: Territorial Politics in Canada and the United States*, (Toronto: Butterworths, 1982).

K. Griffin and J. Gurley, "Radical Analyses of Imperialism, the Third World, and the Transition to Socialism," *Journal of Economic Literature*, (Vol. 23, No. 3, September 1985), pp. 1089-1143.

J.A. Kay and D.J. Thompson, "Privatization: A Policy in Search of a Rationale," *Economic Journal*, (Vol. 96, No. 381, March 1986), pp. 18-32.

R.O. Keohane, *After Hegemony. Co-operation and Discord in the World Political Economy*, (Princeton: Princeton University Press, 1984).

C.P. Kindleberger, *The World in Depression, 1929-1939*, Revised and Enlarged Edition, (Berkeley: University of California Press, 1986).

B. Klein and K.B. Leffler, "The Role of Market Forces in Assuring Contractual Performance," *Journal of Political Economy*, (Vol. 89, No. 4, August 1981), pp. 615-641.

H.E. Leland, "Quacks, Lemons, and Licencing: A Theory of Minimum Quality Standards," *Journal of Political Economy*, (Vol. 87, No. 6, December 1979), pp. 1328-1346.

G.F. Mathewson and R.A. Winter, "The Economics of Franchise Contracts," *Journal of Law and Economics*, (Vol. 28, No. 3, October 1985), pp. 503-526.

W.J. Mommsen, *Theories of Imperialism*, Translated by P.S. Falla, (Chicago: University of Chicago Press, 1977/1982).

R. Nurkse (with W.A. Brown, Jr.,), *International Currency Experience*, (League of Nations, 1944).

W.E. Oates, "The Effects of Property Taxes and Local Spending on Property Values: An Empirical Study of Tax Capitalization and the Tiebout Hypotheses," *Journal of Political Economy*, (Vol. 77, No. 6, November/December 1969), pp. 957-971.

J.F. Reinganum, "Technology Adoption Under Imperfect Information," *Bell Journal of Economics*, Vol. 14, No. 1, Spring, 1983), pp. 57-69.

W.H. Riker and J. Lemco, "The Relation Between Structure and Stability in Federal Governments," in Riker, *The Development of American Federalism*, (Amsterdam: Kluwer Academic Publishers, 1987), pp. 113-129.

R. Romano, "Law as a Product: Some Pieces of the Incorporation Puzzle," *Journal of Law, Economics, and Organization*, (Vol. 1, No. 2, Fall, 1985), pp. 225-283.

Report of the Royal Commission on Dominion-Provincial Relations, (Ottawa: Queen's Printer, 1940).

S. Rose-Ackerman, "Market Models of Local Government: Exit, Voting and the Land Market," *Journal of Urban Economics*, (Vol. 6, No. 3, July, 1979), pp. 319-337.

P. Salmon, "The Logic of Pressure Groups and the Structure of the Public Sector," *European Journal of Political Economy*, (Vol. 3, Nos. 1 & 2, 1987a), pp. 55-86.

P. Salmon, "Decentralization as an Incentive Scheme," *Oxford Review of Economic Policy*, (Vol. 3, No. 2, Summer, 1987b), pp. 24-43.

P.A. Samuelson, "Schumpeter as an Economic Theorist," in H. Frisch, ed., *Schumpeterian Economics*, (London: Praeger, 1982), pp. 1-27.

J.A. Schumpeter, *The Theory of Economic Development*, (New York: Oxford University Press, Galaxy Books, 1911/1961).

J.A. Schumpeter, *Capitalism, Socialism and Democracy*, (New York: Harper and Row, 1942, 1975).

K.A. Shepsle and B.R. Weingast, "Structure-Induced Equilibrium and Legislative Choice," *Public Choice*, (Vol. 37, No. 3, 1981), pp. 503-519.

C. Shapiro, "Premiums for High Quality Products as Returns to Reputations," *Quarterly Journal of Economics*, (Vol. XCVIII, No. 4, November 1983), pp. 659-679.

D.V. Smiley, "The Structural Problem of Canadian Federalism," *Canadian Public Administration*, (Vol. 14, Fall, 1971), pp. 326-343.

J.E. Stiglitz, "The Theory of Local Public Goods," in M.S. Feldstein and R.P. Inman, eds., *The Economics of Public Services*, (London: Macmillan, 1977).

C.M. Tiebout, "A Pure Theory of Local Expenditures," *Journal of Political Economy*, (Vol. 64, No. 5, October 1956), pp. 416-424.

J.L. Walker, "The Diffusion of Innovations Among the American States," *American Political Science Review*, (Vol. 63, No. 3, September 1969), pp. 880-899.

F. Westhoff, "Policy Inferences from Choice Models: A Caution," *Journal of Urban Economics*, (Vol. 6, No. 4, October 1979), pp. 535-549.

O.E. Williamson, "Credible Commitments: Using Hostages to Support Exchange," *American Economic Review*, (Vol. 83, No. 4, September 1983), pp. 519-540.

S. Winer and D. Gauthier, *Internal Migration and Fiscal Structure: An Econometric Study of the Determinants of Interprovincial Migration in Canada*, (Ottawa: Economic Council of Canada, 1982).

R.K. Winter, Jr., "State Law, Shareholder Protection, and the Theory of the Corporation," *Journal of Legal Studies*, (Vol. 6, No. 2, June 1977), pp. 251-292.

COMMENTS
ON ALBERT BRETON'S PAPER

by Edwin G. West, Carleton University
and
Dan Usher, Queen's University

EDWIN G. WEST

I would like to begin with some preliminary observations on the opening example in Albert Breton's paper wherein one country wishes to implement a policy of fiscal expansion but is prevented from so doing by fears of worsening its balance of trade. The argument is that only by international co-operation could such fears be reduced. Indeed all countries could better themselves via co-operation because they could then all effectively implement the appropriate macro policy. The Breton paper focuses on the absence of a robust institutional framework that can make international co-operation possible and it proceeds to explore possible ways of improving that framework. I want to observe merely that, even with the best possible institutional means available for co-operation, there remains much doubt not only about the willingness to undertake it but also about the probable effectiveness of it. For instance several other countries may not like to protect others that want to expand fiscally because, in their opinion, the result will be inflationary; and they may believe that inflation is the worst of all evils. It is such differences in opinion that surely lay behind the current failure of America and Japan to agree on matters of diagnosis.

Again if the issue is cyclical stabilization we must remind ourselves that the record of fiscal policy in this context has not been highly successful in the past, even in individual countries. The problem of discretionary management has been aggravated of course by information time lags, action time lags and lags in the actual impact of stabilization policies on economies. Clearly there is usually room for much difference of opinion about these variables. One can only anticipate that all such difficulties are magnified when transferred to discretionary policy at the world level.

But let us overlook these problems for the moment. Let us agree that some international co-operation is potentially better than none. This brings us to the central proposition of Professor Breton's paper which is that reproducing the conditions of successful federalism internationally could generate greater global stability via feasible co-operation. Like most of Albert's work the ideas here are provocative and challenging, but I detect in this case an unusual inner tension. The paper starts with a somewhat enthusiastic review of the stabilizing properties of federalism within nation states, but the subsequent search for federalist-like institutions at the international level becomes increasingly frustrating, if not pessimistic. The four conditions necessary for the stability of intergovernmental competition are in Breton's words "only very poorly satisfied in the international as compared to the federalist context." The governing politicians in the hegemon for instance, are obviously not elected internationally by citizens across the world. The same politicians' ability, moreover, to simulate the taxing power of a federalist government is very limited and it enjoys no entrenched constitutional powers.

The paper argues that the hegemon will not fulfil its role properly if it is not willing to assume the responsibility of counteracting world instability. It is not entirely clear to me why any such government would want to adopt such responsibility. But as an Englishman, I must say I find it difficult to resist the idea that in the past Great Britain did rise to the occasion and that the world became somewhat chaotic after that country's decline.

Albert Breton regrets that the United States is not the hegemonic power that it used to be and that if we have any hope for stability of competition internationally it must rest on the possibility of successful co-operation between regimes. He admits that the task of reproducing the four conditions for stability that prevail in federal states is formidable. He concedes, for instance, that the probability that some power to tax will be assigned to a central world authority is now nil. And as for representation of the interests of peripheral citizens, we find the most ominous possibility awaiting us. Officials in international regimes are not elected to represent directly the interests of a "far-flung" electorate. But if co-operation fails to reflect the preferences and interests of the internationally spread population, Breton tells us, "it degenerates into collusion which is probably worse than some degree of competitive instability."

It is recognized then that competitive instability after all is not necessarily the worst thing that can happen to us. To me, this insight is just as important as the others in the Breton Paper. But what I want to stress is that if collusion within single government systems involves substantial costs, then collusion across all governments could raise them exponentially.

To what extent does collusion occur between governments in America's federal system? If collusion can be demonstrated to be serious in that system, there may be a flaw in the central pillar of the present paper's argument. This is because the paper takes federalism, especially American federalism, as the inspiration for reform at the international level. Now not all economists portray federalism in the way that Professor Breton does. Consider, for instance, his fourth condition: the argument that for federal systems to succeed, the central government must be allowed to allocate intergovernmental grants and to undertake regional policies. It is interesting to compare an entirely different line of analysis. In their book *The Power to Tax* (1980), Brennan and Buchanan examine the possibility that the central federal government in the U.S. acts as monitor of a cartel among lower levels of government. In the face of widespread potential ability of citizens to "vote with their feet," there are constant pressures by lower-level governments to secure institutional rearrangements that deliberately weaken the competition between them.

One way, of course, for a member government to compete is for it to lower its tax rates relative to other member governments' rates in order to attract a larger proportion of the national population. To stop this, a pattern of fiscal federalism can emerge that serves primarily the objective of a cartel of member governments. One arrangement would be to establish a uniform tax system across all jurisdictions. The central government could then be used as the enforcer of the cartel agreement between lower-level governments. To curb those jurisdictions that are tempted to breach the agreement, substantial financial penalties could be arranged. One method of doing this is to allocate the share of total revenue going to each lower-level government according to the degree of its "fiscal effort." Another prediction is that the governmental benefits from the cartelization would be shared more or less equally across states or provinces. This is because any lower-level government unit could effectively break the cartel by remitting taxes and attempting thereby to attract extra residents. It is in *this* sense, according to Brennan and Buchanan, that we ought to expect small states or provinces to obtain bigger per capita shares than large states.

To Brennan and Buchanan revenue sharing, or the program of equalization payments as it is known in Canada, is undesirable because it subverts the primary purpose of federalism, which is to *create* competition between jurisdictions. Albert Breton's view, in contrast, is that one of the functions of federalism is to *control* such competition. For him, competition is a problem because it leads to instability.

In the most recent empirical literature the Brennan and Buchanan thesis appears to be gaining much attention. Marlow (1988) reports strong and consistent evidence that increases in the share of state and local expenditures in total government expenditures in the U.S. are positively correlated with reductions in total public sector size. These results, he considers, offer support for the use of monopoly government assumptions in public policy models.

Grossman (1989) extends Marlow's analysis by examining the impact that collusive actions between central and lower level governments have on total government size. His evidence is consistent with the hypothesis that the effectiveness of federalist decentralization as a device for controlling governmental growth is hindered by a system of intergovernmental grants.

Finally, with reference to Breton's citation of particular models of destabilizing mobility, these are based on special circumstances. One could argue, first, that the given circumstances may not always prevail, or second, that it is possible to cite other models (e.g. Henderson 1985) that do not predict instability. But even if one is persuaded that geographical mobility leads to instability, we still have to come back to Albert Breton's conjecture that government collusion could be an even worse problem. In other words, we may still face a trade-off between instability and government inefficiency. I simply conclude by saying that, if the Brennan/Buchanan view of revenue sharing is realistic, as recent empirical studies suggest, and if most governments act like cartels, then paving the way for international co-operation between them will so compound the problem of collusion that the policy becomes counterproductive and should therefore be avoided.

REFERENCES

J. Vernon Henderson: "The Tiebout Model: Bring back the Entrepreneurs," *Journal of Political Economy*, 1985.

M.L. Marlow, "Fiscal decentralization and government size," *Public Choice* 56, pp. 259-270, 1988.

Philip Grossman, "Federalism and the Size of Government," *Southern Economic Journal* 55, 3, pp. 580-593, January 1989.

DAN USHER

To what extent might Canadian federalism serve as a model for world government? That is not quite the question that Breton poses, but it is close enough to merit a brief comment. The question is whether the Canadian accommodations to jurisdictional spillovers might serve as a basis for international co-operation or for the establishment of a federal government world wide.

Intergovernmental rivalry may be socially beneficial like competition among firms in a market, or it may be destructive like self-interested behaviour in a prisoners' dilemma. The core of Breton's paper is an analysis of intergovernmental rivalry to assess its consequence for the organization of provinces within a country and countries within the world. Breton examines three important instances of jurisdictional spillovers: (a) *Demonstration effects* in which socially desirable policies in one country are copied in another because the political party in power in the copying country knows that it would be displaced otherwise. This is a desirable form of intergovernmental rivalry. It is a prisoners' dilemma among political parties in different countries, but not, of course, among citizens in these countries. (Recall that, in the classic prisoners' dilemma, it is only the prisoners who lose by confession; the rest of the population may well gain from keeping the prisoners locked up for a good long time.) (b) *Intergovernmental rivalry over fiscal policy* where, by assumption, expansion might be beneficial to all countries simultaneously but no country dare expand alone for fear of the impact upon its balance of payments; (c) *The race for the bottom* in the design by state of corporation law, where it may be beneficial for the nation as a whole to maintain strict rules over the administration of the corporation — rules pertaining to such matters as disclosure of information to stockholders, rights of executives and members of boards of directors to use the revenue of the firm to fight off contestants for control, insider trading, dealings among closely connected firms and so on — but where each state has an interest in attracting incorporations through the establishment of rules that are very favourable to the management of the firm. To these might be added several other sources of interjurisdictional economic conflict; (d) *Spillovers in taxation* where it is in the interest of all jurisdictions to maintain substantial rates of sales tax as long as these rates are the same everywhere but where each jurisdiction has an incentive to maintain rates lower than those in neighbouring jurisdictions to attract customers from across its borders; and (e) *Free riding on provision to the poor* where every-body wants to see the destitute supported to some extent but each local-ity, in a society where provision for the poor is a local rather than a central responsibility, has an incentive to keep its own rate of provision somewhat lower than that in neighbouring localities so as to induce the poor to settle elsewhere. This last source of interjurisdictional conflict might be called the "Vermont" problem as distinct from the "Delaware" problem concerning the specification of rules of behaviour for the corporation. The problem is pervasive; politicians who advocate decentralized pro-vision for the poor are either naïve as to the effects of such policies or using advocacy of decentralization as a way of indicating that they would like to see provisions reduced, without actually saying so. More directly, jurisdictions come into conflict over (f) *Trade policy* as when Great Britain went to war with China over China's unwillingness to allow free trade in all commodities, and (g) *Ownership of territory or people.*

It remains unclear to me what Breton means by "instability." The word may refer to a Pareto inferior outcome in which co-operation policies by all jurisdictions could make everybody better off, or to the absence of any Nash equilibrium so that jurisdictions keep changing policies for-ever in response to changes by other jurisdictions, or to a situation where jurisdictions become so exasperated with one another that they resort to war. None of these outcomes are desirable and all may perhaps be avoided through domination by one jurisdiction over another, through explicit co-operation among formally independent jurisdictions or through fed-eralism in which a central government occupies powers over aspects in the economy where interjurisdictional conflict of interest is likely to be most severe. Breton leans towards federalism as the most that can rea-sonably be expected of international government at this time. To what extent can this prescription, which is certainly appropriate for Canada, be administered to the world at large?

Breton is right in asserting that federalism requires a number of im-portant powers to be invested in the central government, first among these being the monopoly of the means of violence through the control of the army. This however is precisely the source of the major obstacle to world government: the universal, and unfortunately justified, fear on the part of the would-be citizens that the world army will be employed in the interest of a ruling class or an elected majority from which they are ex-cluded. Here Canadian federalism is at best an imperfect model for world government, for the factors that lessen these fears within Canada are to some degree unique to Canada and not easily reproducible on a larger scale. The temptation on the part of the group forming the government to use its authority to expropriate income from the rest of the population is always less when the initial distribution of income and property is narrow than when the initial distribution is wide, for there is less to gain from redistribution and less willingness to risk the inefficiency and the undermining of political institutions that a massive redistribution would generate. There should be less fear of exploitation in a federation encompassing Prince Edward Island and Alberta than in a federation encompassing Canada and Ethiopia, where each person has one vote and the army is ultimately at the behest of the majority of citizens. Furthermore, the great cultural division that does exist between French and English is contained, insofar as it is contained at all, partly by a consensus about property rights and partly by a general understanding that Canada as we know it is not worth preserving if the preservation of the country requires the use of violence against the occupants of any large region that wishes to separate. The splitting of a country is no great matter in a world already composed of many independent countries, but it is logically inconsistent with world government.

Chapter III   D 2 3

ORIGINS OF THEORIES
OF ORGANIZATION:
THE COMMON PROPERTY ROOT

* Keith Acheson and Stephen Ferris, Carleton University

Economic models typically focus on the equilibrium consumption and production flows of a frictionless world. In these models, the decision makers are firms and households which are imposed as axiomatic constructs. By assumption, the analysis cannot explain the existence of such organizations nor the nature of resource allocation and dispute resolution within them. A solution to a set of equations reflecting agents' choices under the constraints of technology, price-taking, and "markets" for outputs and factors clearing states the result of co-ordinating the economy. From a behavioural story describing the assumptions embodied in the equations and the process of solving them, the solution is labelled a "competitive-market" or "price-system" equilibrium. Much attention has been paid to the existence, uniqueness and stability of the solution. With the exception of the representation of the tatonnement process as a mechanism for finding the equilibrium prices, the process of co-ordination received little attention. In the traditional literature, firms and markets participate in an "immaculate" co-ordination in which their operation absorbs no resources.

More recently the economic problem of co-ordinating activity within an institution and among institutions and individuals has been directly addressed. While general analytical contributions exist in this literature, many important insights have emerged from detailed studies of specific

*   Much of what we have to say has been influenced positively by John McManus. We thank Tom Borcherding for his insightful comments, and the conference organizer, T.K. Rymes, for the opportunity to pay our respects to Scott and his scholarship.

organizational problems. The seminal ideas in organizational analysis have often been expressed and analyzed verbally and the concepts have sometimes defied mathematical modelling.

In this paper, we provide a guided tour of some of the core ideas in the theory of organization. A comprehensive examination of this literature reveals the following insights: the importance of exclusion as revealed by the common property right problem; the recognition of transaction costs as a necessary condition for the existence of an organizational problem; asymmetric information as the ultimate source of transactions costs; and the analytical insight that different institutions have comparative advantages in minimizing the sum of production and transactions costs. Each strand has complex elements and a number of off shoots. To keep our paper manageable we do not address the source of transactions costs, but focus on the other aspects.[1] Even here our tour provides only a selective history of certain central ideas and discusses their profound implications for applied price theory.

THE COMMON PROPERTY RIGHT

The starting point for our analysis is the 1924 paper by Frank Knight on the common property right problem. In that paper Knight criticized Pigou's claim that diminishing return industries were "too large," hence corrective taxes should be applied. Using an example of two roads, a broad one with constant marginal costs and a narrow one with rising marginal costs, Knight showed that competitive use of the two roads resulted in the equality of their average costs in equilibrium. Use of the narrow road was "excessive," but the problem was not rising costs *per se*. A tax was warranted only if no one owned the narrow road:

> If the roads are assumed to be subject to private appropriation and exploitation, precisely the ideal situation which would be established by the imaginary tax will be brought about through the operation of ordinary economic motives. The owner of the broad road could not under effective competition charge anything for its use. If an agency of production is not subject to diminishing returns, and cannot be monopolized, there is, in fact, no incentive to its appropriation, and it will remain a free good. But the owner of the narrow road can charge for its use a toll representing its "superiority" over the free road, in accordance with the theory of rent, which is as old as Ricardian economics. An application of

the familiar reasoning to this case will show that the toll will
exactly equal the ideal tax... (Knight, 1924, pp. 163-4.)

The common property congestion problem is, of course, no more than
a reciprocal externality problem. Without a rationing device on the narrow road, additional users cause the costs of other travellers to rise once
a certain level of traffic is reached. At first the impact on others is more
than offset by the advantage experienced by the incremental user
switching from the broad road to the narrow. Social wealth rises despite
the interaction. The interaction becomes dissipative of social wealth only
when the additional user gains less than the damages imposed on existing users, i.e. when marginal cost on the narrow road exceeds the marginal
cost on the broad road. If an appropriate rationing device is used, congestion costs are internalized and there is no externality in equilibrium.
The applicability of the analysis of the common property right problem
to organizational issues was not immediately apparent. In writing his
article, Knight was interested in showing the importance that private
property played in determining the efficacy of the price system, a topic
which he considered to be the dominant issue in economics.

> If economic theory is interpreted as a critique of the com-
> petitive system of organization, its first and most general
> problem is that of determining whether the fundamental ten-
> dencies of free contractual relations under competitive control
> lead to the maximum production of value as measured in price
> terms. (Knight, 1924, p. 161.)

Knight had not immersed himself in a comparative organizational study
of how roads could be provided, but created his example to illustrate a
point in logic implicitly assuming no transactions cost. In this setting, if
private property rights exist, Pigou's problem will disappear. If they are
absent, creating them will provide a remedy as effective as Pigou's tax.
Pigou may have recommended one remedy and Knight another. However, in the absence of transactions costs, the respective recommendations reflect a taste for the instrument and not a dispute over consequences.
The important inference from the debate is that the common property
right problem disappears with an understanding of its nature and the application of one among many remedies.

Professional attention was not drawn back to the common property
problem until Scott Gordon (1954) analyzed the problem of the fishery
some 30 years later. He addressed what was then known about the interaction of fishing effort, the catch and the stock of fish,[2] and concluded that

concern for "conservation" and fear of "depletion" or "overexploitation" of the fishery reflected the common property of the fishing ground. With characteristic crispness, Gordon provided the following description of the problem:

> Common-property natural resources are free goods for the individual and scarce goods for society. Under unregulated private exploitation, they can yield no rent; that can be accomplished only by methods which can make them private property or public (government) property, in either case subject to a unified directing power. (1954, p. 135.)

Gordon emphasized that having the right to exclude, to limit access, is crucial to correcting the problem. The ownership of the right is irrelevant as long as the right can be transferred costlessly. Without introducing transactions cost Gordon's statement of the problem left the reader at the same point as Knight had, i.e. depletion or overexploitation results from the lack of exclusion by an owner through private or public levies.

However, embedded in Gordon's account was an awareness of the costliness of exclusion under different arrangements. Unlike Knight, Gordon was deeply immersed in the specific details of his problem, the fishery, and aware of the manner in which transactions costs had manifested themselves in the different organizational solutions that had been tried. His accounts indicated that restricting access to realize the potential of the fishery was far from easy. For example, with respect to the catch limit for Pacific halibut, he noted:

> Since the method of control was to halt fishing when the limit had been reached, this created a great incentive on the part of each fisherman to get the fish before his competitors. During the last twenty years, fishermen have invested in more, larger, and faster boats in a competitive race for fish.... What has been happening is a rise in the average cost of fishing effort, allowing no gap between average production and average cost to appear, and hence no rent. (1954. p. 133.)

In this case, Gordon describes the reappearance of the common property right problem in the context of an apparent solution to the original manifestation of the problem. Crowding along the time dimension was dissipating all the potential rent derived from limiting the catch.

A similar point was made with respect to the Canadian Atlantic Coast lobster conservation program which was regulated by imposing seasonal closure.

...The result has been a steady growth in the number of lobster
traps set by each fisherman. Virtually all available lobsters
are now caught each year within the season, but at much
greater cost in gear and supplies. At a fairly conservative es-
timate, the same quantity of lobsters could be caught with
half the present number of traps. (Gordon, 1954, p. 134.)

Again, the solution is plagued by another version of the common property right problem — "too many" along an undisciplined margin, which
in this case is traps rather than fishermen. In addition, Gordon went beyond fishing to describe how the common property problem had manifested itself in the oil industry and how oil regulation underwent a tatonnement that developed successively better control mechanisms.[3]

That the common property right problem can exist as an *equilibrium*
phenomenon, and not just as a temporary aberration reflecting the lack
of understanding of policy makers, was implicit in Gordon's discussion
of primitive societies:

Significantly, land tenure is found to be "common" only in
those cases where the hunting resource is migratory over such
large areas that it cannot be regarded as husbandable by the
society. (1954, p. 134.)

An evolutionary theory of institutions similar to that later developed by
Demsetz (1967) and McManus (1972) was also outlined in Gordon's
discussion of mechanisms adopted by primitive societies to curb dissipation arising from the common property problem.

Speaking generally, we may say that stable primitive cultures appear to have discovered the dangers of common-
property tenure and to have developed measures to protect
their resources. Or, if a more Darwinian explanation be preferred, we may say that only those primitive cultures have
survived which succeeded in developing such institutions.
(Gordon, 1954, pp. 134-135.)

Gordon's article reflects a tension between the theoretical analysis of
a world of no transaction costs and the world he observed. Although he
never mentions transaction costs explicitly, Gordon describes situations
and choices which are made meaningful only by their existence. All his
examples involve instances where property rights are clearly incompletely
specified: hunting, fishing, medieval commons, or the common oil pool.
Nevertheless, the seed of a generalization to all transactions is there. By
noting the difficulties in controlling access in these cases, attention is

drawn to an organizational problem, the costs of excluding, which affects the exercise of all rights. Whatever the system of organization, from unencumbered private property to government regulation, exclusion is necessary to increase wealth and is attainable only at a cost.

COASE AND INSTITUTIONAL COMPARATIVE ADVANTAGE

Coase was the first to recognize explicitly the costs of transacting in determining institutional form. Institutions expanded or contracted or were replaced according to the same economic logic that applied to the production of goods and services. With respect to the firm, he noted:

> At the margin, the costs of organizing within the firm will be equal either to the costs of organizing in another firm or to the costs involved in leaving the transaction to be "organised" by the price mechanism. (Coase, 1937, p. 350.)

There would be a similar margin between activities organized by the firm and by government regulation.

> In the standard case of a smoke nuisance, which may affect a vast number of people engaged in a wide variety of activities, the administrative costs might well be so high as to make any attempt to deal with the problem within the confines of a single firm impossible. An alternative solution is direct Government regulation. Instead of instituting a legal system of rights which can be modified by transactions on the market, the government may impose regulations which state what people must or must not do and which have to be obeyed. (Coase, 1960, p. 17.)

Comparative advantage in coping with the costs of organization determines institutional structure.

In a world with transactions costs, Coase's words and more importantly the logic of his argument suggest that competition among alternative institutions and organizational forms will generate more efficient outcomes. This point is worth emphasizing since the contrary view that Coase's arguments are designed to justify laissez faire and are antithetical to government regulation is often asserted. For example, in a recent article Farrell[4] states:

> But while Coase suggested that the efficiency of ideal bargaining means that everything can be decentralized, the mechanism-design view is that it means the opposite: centralization lets us have such a process (through an ex-

pected-externality scheme) while we know that decentralized bargaining is imperfect when there is private information. (1987, p. 119.)

With private information transacting is costly. In this world Coase did not claim unconditional superiority for decentralized bargaining. To do so would have made nonsense of his theory of the firm and for his view that the courts play an efficient allocative role in a world of transactions costs. Farrell contends that he is contradicting Coase when he illustrates that there are situations where "the king's power to coerce really helps to achieve efficiency." (1987, p. 120.) In doing so, however, Farrell merely repeats a point made by Coase 27 years earlier. Coase noted that the state has:

> at its disposal the police and the other law enforcement agencies to make sure that its regulations are carried out.
>
> It is clear that the government has the powers which might enable it to get some things done at a lower cost than could a private organisation (or at any rate one without special governmental powers). (1960, p. 17.)

Coase's position is that the comparative advantage of different institutional form is an empirical rather than a theoretical or ideological matter. Coase's preference for "market" solutions in a transactions costly world does not follow from his theory. Rather, it derives from his interpretation of what empirical work on organization has revealed.

Coase's conclusions here seem more debatable. In 1988, Coase wrote that regulation by specialized tribunals has had adverse results[5] and that there is a *prima facie* case against intervention rather than for it. He also concluded that

> the studies on the effects of regulation which have been made in recent years in the United States, ranging from agriculture to zoning, ... indicate that regulation has commonly made matters worse. (1988d, p. 26.)

It seems ironic that the same Coase who admonishes "blackboard" economists for advocating remedies that require more information than is available is willing to draw such a strong conclusion from "blackboard" empirical studies. Given the logic of his argument, a greater emphasis on the survival record in the political and economic market seems more appropriate. No doubt many economists have different priors on the efficacy of intervention and might assess American empirical studies differently.[6] Nevertheless, disagreements over the significance of empirical findings or ideological priors should not obscure the importance of Coase's proposition that there is no theoretical mechanism for ranking the efficiency of organizational form independent of the transaction situation.

In resolving externalities, Coase emphasized the interaction of costs across agents. Like Knight, he was generally critical of Pigou's tax remedies.[7] Coase's concern was that the tax would fail to maximize wealth in cases where it provided corrective incentives for only some of the contributing parties.[8]

ZERO TRANSACTIONS COSTS AND TRADITIONAL PRICE THEORY

To illustrate the central proposition that transactions costs are a necessary condition for legal decisions to have efficiency implications, Coase began by examining a world in which "the price system is assumed to work without cost." (1960, p. 8.) What precisely is meant by a world of zero transactions costs is not clear. For our purposes, we assume that mechanisms exist that costlessly make all information about resources available to all individuals. All promises are also costlessly enforceable. For public goods, the unanimity principle rules.[9] Complex contracts are costless to make and enforce. Strategic disputes over rents are costlessly resolved. In this world, an optimal allocation of resources will result from contract and exchange, subject only to the caveat that a voluntary solution exists that is robust against "separatist" coalitions, i.e. that a core exists.[10]

For rights to be transferred in exchange to their most highly valued use, they must be delineated and allocated among individuals. This may be done by a *deus ex machina* who decides on an original distribution, or by a social contract where individuals agree to establish mechanisms that permit wealth generation and its distribution.

INCOME DISTRIBUTION AND TRANSACTION COSTS

In the Coasean zero-transactions cost world described above, trading plans can be made over all contingencies and all time periods on day one. It is similar to, but more general than, an Arrow-Debreu complete markets price-taking world, since deals may be complex and imply non-linear prices. Contractual agreements exhaust gains from transferring goods, resources and risk; there can be no further surprises, only realizations.

The original assignment of rights could include a state-dependent redistribution scheme, whereby rights are reassigned subject to different contingencies. In a transactions costless world, such schemes will not affect the efficiency with which resources are combined. This is because knowledge of the details of the redistribution scheme from day one means that its effects will be fully reflected in subsequent contracts. An individual who wishes to contract to use resource i, in period j, for each possible state 1,..., k, will now have contingent contracts with all the owners of the right in the various states, with ownership determined by the distribution scheme. Similarly the individual's initial wealth is measured by the value of his or her endowment of state-contingent rights. The effects of an ongoing redistribution scheme that is anticipated will then be perfectly reflected in the initial value of endowments. Conversely, all income redistribution objectives could be achieved on day one by an ownership of state conditional rights.

Individual risk is affected by a state contingent income redistribution scheme, but social risk is not. Costless markets transfer individual risk efficiently. Unanticipated redistributions are ruled out by assumption. Moreover, income redistribution schemes which do not alter the state contingent ownership or rights but, for example, tax or subsidize discretionary variables will distort incentives and cause inefficiency. This means that when zero transactions costs are generalized to community decisions, the Wicksellian unanimity requirement will rule out inefficient tax and subsidy redistribution schemes, as well as inefficient rights structures.[11]

As soon as transactions costs are introduced, organizational comparative advantage can be determined only through a detailed knowledge of the transacting environment. Defining all the conditional rights of individuals in innumerable states, of which only one will be realized, can be prohibitively expensive. Exchange will realize only a portion of the potential gains achievable in a zero transactions cost world. Redistribution mechanisms that were dominated in the absence of transactions costs may now become efficient. In these circumstances, it is conceivable that a specified process for reassigning existing rights and creating new ones may be preferred to market exchange with no redistribution of rights or definition of new rights. If this is the case, exchange and "allocating by process" become substitutes at some margin. Coase perceives Anglo-American Common Law in this light:

> ...the situation is quite different when market transactions
> are so costly as to make it difficult to change the arrangement
> of rights established by law. In such cases, the courts directly
> influence economic activity. It would therefore seem desirable
> that the courts should understand the economic consequences
> of their decisions and should, insofar as this is possible with-

out creating too much uncertainty about the legal position itself, take these consequences into account when making their decisions. (Coase, 1960, p. 19.)

In a world of transactions costs, Coase's caveat about the uncertainties created by court ordered reallocations of rights requires elaboration.

Consider the fishery. As Gordon noted "... fish in the sea are value-less to the fisherman, because there is no assurance that they will be there tomorrow if they are left behind today" (1954, p. 425.) Suppose, however, that technological change makes exclusion from the fishery feasible and private property rights are introduced. Transferring the right, however, is costly. There are then a number of mutually exclusive uses of the fishery associated with different sets of individuals using the right where the value of these alternative uses is state dependent. If the court can observe the states of nature, the court can improve efficiency by assigning use to the group which generates most value (transactions cost make reassignment uneconomic to achieve through the market[12]). How-ever, if husbanding the fish stock will raise value across all uses and if it is too costly for potential future users to pay current incumbents to con-sider the future fish stock, the fish stock will be less nurtured than in a situation in which the current user maintained ownership across all states. Overall, if improved husbanding of the fish stock with secure ownership would outweigh the gain from shifting use with changes in ownership, the court should eschew redistribution on efficiency grounds.

A court instructed to maximize economic wealth could then envision effects along all dimensions and determine an appropriate allocation of rights. To do so, however, it would have to process much information. Presumably, the same forces that make the parties unable to realize an economical means of transferring ownership of the fishing ground will affect the attempts of the justices to do so. Basically, the efficiency argu-ment for court reassignment of rights depends on the ability of the courts to deal with the barriers to co-ordination at lower cost than the market.[13] Is the judge better than the auctioneer? Coase did not examine the basis of this comparative advantage in detail.[14] More generally, it is difficult to understand how the course of action prescribed for the judiciary dif-fers at all from the course of action required to implement the tax proposals of a Pigouvian "interventionist."

The fishery example illustrates that the court's efforts to place the rights in the hands of the most highly valued user of the moment will be prone to the same types of "failures" that Gordon had noted as characteristic of the regulatory schemes in the fishery. A "common property problem" will re-emerge along another dimension, dissipating at least some of the gain produced by correcting the initial margin. Coase was aware of the complexity of organizational problems and, as a general warning, stated:

> Analysis in terms of divergencies between private and social products concentrates attention on particular deficiencies in the system and tends to nourish the belief that any measure which will remove the deficiency is necessarily desirable. It diverts attention from those other changes in the system which are inevitably associated with the corrective measure, changes which may well produce more harm than the original deficiency. (Coase, 1960, p. 43.)

His generally unqualified support of a role for the courts in reassigning rights is inconsistent with this stricture.

The proposition that courts are superior from an efficiency perspective to private or other public institutions is made even more problematic by the high probability that a sequence of decisions rather than a single one is involved. The constant discovery of unanticipated effects and necessity of subsequent readjustments means that the ultimate arrival at a remedial arrangement to an organizational problem through private arrangement or through government regulation will be a process rather than an isolated event. To describe the process in the private sphere, Oliver Williamson has introduced the concept of a governance structure, an umbrella of understood rules and procedures that constrain and direct a process. In the public sphere, some authors (e.g. Goldberg, 1976; Williamson, 1976) have characterized regulation as a contract involving sequential adjustment to circumstances. That the traditional courts are equipped to govern effectively a dynamic process of adjustments is questionable.[15]

The courts can contribute to reducing transactions costs from "gaming" or "rent-seeking" by parties involved in value-creating processes through providing an alternative and predictable resolution mechanism to bargaining. Because this mechanism will be, in our opinion, more expensive than bargaining, parties would normally eschew it in favour of bargaining. The court option however reduces bargaining costs by narrowing the set of mutually advantageous solutions.

The case for court participation is stronger with the creation of new rights than in the reassignment of existing rights.[16] In this case, a court decision does not jeopardize security of tenure in existing rights, although it does affect their value. The decision also creates the incentive to husband and care and permits the realization of gains from exchange.

With both the creation and reassignment of rights, if income redistribution is anticipated, incentives will be affected. Given the spirit of Coase's approach, it is surprising that the courts would choose to impose a new regime with a different wealth configuration.[17] That the courts do not simulate "the bargain that might have been" raises the question of whether equity considerations are not side effects but determining factors in legal decisions.

That the courts participate in determining the political distributional equilibrium would not be surprising. In democracies, judges are usually agents of governments, although in some jurisdictions, they are directly elected. Typically, the appointment procedure and the terms of appointment are established by custom or constitution to provide some degree of independence. Nevertheless, one would expect the political ramifications of a decision's impact on redistribution to influence the court.

Several authors have argued that an "invisible hand" directs court decisions towards efficiency. They model the competitive behaviour of the litigants and the courts. For example, the initiation of a court case may depend on the interest of each party in the action itself and in setting favourable precedents. The decisions of the courts may depend on precedents and the investments of the parties in the litigation, or on some random mechanism.[18] If the resulting decisions are expected to be inferior to an alternative form of redress for the initiating party, the legal process will not be chosen. Only efficient legal processes will survive while the inefficient ones will wither away.

In these models, if a process is chosen and survives, it is revealed to be efficient. Survivability does not allow an observer to determine whether the objective of the courts is to pursue efficiency alone or a combination of efficiency and income redistribution. If both "equity" and efficiency were being pursued, survivability would indicate no better process for pursuing these two attributes.

From his examination of British court cases, Coase concluded that the courts were in fact guided by the efficiency effects of their decisions.[19]

> ...they often make, although not always in a very explicit fashion, a comparison between what would be gained and what lost by preventing actions which have harmful effects. (Coase 1960, p. 28.)

Coase does not document the degree to which equity considerations influence British court decisions, with one interesting exception. In a case where the court forced a fried fish shop serving relatively poor customers to move because it was a nuisance to some nearby rich residents, he reports:

> Had there been no other more "suitable place in the neighbourhood," the case would have been more difficult and the decision might have been different. What would the poor people have had for food? No English judge would have said: "Let them eat cake." (Coase, 1960, p. 22.)

The redistributive aspect of legal decisions deserves more attention. Clearly the courts have been influenced by public opinion with respect to the fairness of distributions. For example, at the same time as (and in some cases before) governments in Canada were altering statutes governing rights to property on the dissolution of marriages, court decisions were moving in the same direction (Knetsch, 1984). The motivation was not exclusively to correct inefficiencies but also to reduce inequities or what were perceived as inequities by the polity.[20]

MONOPOLY, COMPETITION AND TRANSACTION COSTS

Institutions play no efficiency role in a transactions costless world, since deals need not be framed within any particular structure. Neither do structural considerations like competition or monopoly. In most general equilibrium models, numbers have nothing to do with the proof of the existence of a solution, but are introduced ex-model as a comment to make price-taking behaviour credible. As Barzel and Kochin write:

> The Coase Theorem, however, holds under more general conditions than those underlying the Walrasian model: it is not derived from any assumption about competition. It must hold, therefore, regardless of the number of players. Thus, when property rights are well defined, the distortions associated with monopoly are absent. This is not a well known result. (Barzel and Kochin, 1968, 8.)

In the Coasean transactions costless world, an owner of a monopoly right undertakes the joint-wealth maximizing allocation and forces terms on customers, either through multi-part prices or all-or-nothing deals, which make them indifferent between dealing and not dealing. Perfect price discrimination is possible since conditions barring resale are costlessly enforceable. If all goods were monopolized, the total expenditures of customers would represent the surplus measure of utility. Measured GNP will be different in the world where monopoly rights exist for all goods, but welfare need not. If wealth effects cancel, allocations will remain the same even if the initial wealth distribution is altered.

Monopoly becomes an efficiency issue only in a world of transactions costs.[21] In the analysis of simple monopoly in conventional price theory, only some transactions costs are assumed to be zero. The exceptions are that it is prohibitively costly for the customers to buy the monopoly right and it is prohibitively costly for the monopolist to determine individual demand curves or prevent resale. This selective, *typically implicit*, introduction of transactions costs is characteristic of conventional price theory. Examining the problem caused by a single seller from a more symmetric transactions cost perspective provides some useful insights.

Once we are in a world of transactions costs, the exclusivity that is championed by Knight and Gordon as a requirement of efficiency, becomes a two-edged sword. In a transactions costly situation, the monopolist may artificially enhance scarcity in an effort to minimize the loss of private surplus caused by the inability to make a deal with the most valued users, the customers. The substitution of scarcity for more direct ways of transferring surplus results in the welfare loss associated with the traditional monopoly solution.

The problem of monopoly is assumed away by both Knight and Gordon. Knight avoids the traditional monopoly problem associated with exclusive ownership of the narrow road, because the existence of the broad road forces price-taking behaviour on any prospective owner of the narrow road. Similarly, Gordon assumes that the market for fish is price-taking. If the domain over which exclusivity must be exercised for efficiency reasons is small so that a number of like assets are created, the price-taking assumption for the output produced by the assets is credible.[22] However, an owner of a fishery or a road usually has some market power resulting from a locational advantage with respect to its customers. Moreover, a fishery that is one among many with respect to marketing fish may have monopsony power with respect to its input markets — the fishermen on its shores. In many of Coase's examples, local monopoly power was bilateral.[23]

The fishermen or travellers facing monopsony or monopoly power in a truly transactions costless world would not gain or lose by owning the fishery or the road. Any owner of the right would elicit a flow of rents equal to the surplus stripped from the consumers. The consumers could internalize this by buying the right but the cost would just equal the benefit. There would be no tendency for consumers' wealth holdings to echo their consumption patterns. If transactions costs exist, the first analytical step suggested by the Coasean approach is to examine the extent to which transactions costs are minimized by different schemes for its resolution. In some instances, ownership by customers may be the most economic way of reducing the welfare loss from the exercise of monopsony power. With the exception of enclosed roads with limited access (and differentiated pricing), it is common for roads to be owned collectively and fishing co-operatives have often been given exclusive rights over local fisheries.[24]

Revealing appropriate remedies for problems of market structure is illustrative of the analytical benefit derived from making transactions costs explicit and the focus of industrial organization analysis. Posing the problem of market structure in its traditional monopoly form unnecessarily restricts the possible solution set to divestiture remedies, regulation of price or a hands-off approach. In the traditional approach, the dichotomy between zero transactions costs in some dimensions and prohibitive ones in others prevents search for remedies along the dimensions ruled out by transacting assumptions.[25]

To approach an organizational problem in this general manner requires a detailed knowledge of the specifics of the problem and a deep understanding of the informational factors generating transactions costs. Since in a transactions costly world almost any trade practice may have an efficiency defence, the analysis and ranking is not an easy task.[26] In addition, the comparison of remedies requires calculation of total benefits under each regime rather than an examination of what is happening at the margin for each remedy.

In the previous sections, the complexity of private and public arrangements necessary to cope with the many dimensions along which wealth can be dissipated was revealed. The transactions cost approach permits a recognition of the need for multi-dimensional solutions or, where these are too costly to construct, for an adaptive process of governance. Ironically, while transactions costs are needed for combines or anti-trust policy to have a rationale, they also increase the cost of discerning the appropriate remedial strategy.

CONCLUSION: TRANSACTIONS COSTS AND TRADITIONAL PRICE THEORY

Traditional free enterprise economists embraced Coase's message about a transactions costless world. In this world, government is subject to unanimity and courts are restricted to enforcing voluntary agreements and the right to exclude. Transactions cost turns this world upside down. The common property right analysis reveals that competition can be excessive, can be bad, and needs to be socially controlled. Transactions costs are necessary to justify political decisions by majority rule and other non-unanimity voting schemes [c.f. Buchanan and Tullock (1962)] for efficiency rather than ideological reasons. The recognition of transactions costs makes industrial organization a more difficult yet richer discipline, one that requires more than simply knowledge of perfectly competitive and simple monopoly models. Its framework provides the possibility of an efficiency defence for government involvement in the economy and thus permits analysis to come to grips with real world institutions and practice. The hypothesis that the price system is the efficient solution to a social co-ordination problem is now replaced with a more agnostic message:

> When an economist is comparing alternative social arrangements, the proper procedure is to compare the total social product yielded by these different arrangements. (Coase 1960, p. 34.)

This message directs attention towards alternative forms of organizations such as co-operatives, governments, the internal structure of firms, and bureaucracies. All of these areas had been ignored in the traditional framework.

That government regulation can be efficient, that rent-seeking may be an unavoidable cost of the most efficient way of making political decisions, that competition needs to be controlled and directed, and that courts can be active in redistributing wealth and replacing market mechanisms for efficiency reasons were not particularly palatable messages for the traditional economist, including the authors of this article, to absorb let alone embrace.[27] However, the logic of analysis that begins with the common property problem and runs through the work of Knight, Gordon and Coase has drawn attention to the importance of observing institutions and conventions and provided a framework for doing so. The resulting insights promise to make the profession more relevant.

While our route through this literature has ended with Coase, the transition to Coase would have been difficult without the insights of Scott Gordon. The generality of the common property problem and multiplicity of the potential efficiency solutions are the first steps in understanding the modern theories of organization.

NOTES

[1]   Insightful treatments are provided in Barzel (1985), McManus (1975) and Williamson (1985).

[2]   More recently, optimal control techniques have been applied to the problem of determining the optimal harvest. These analyses reveal the capital stock aspects of the fish stock, the related importance of the interest rate in determining harvests, as well as the shadow prices of access to the fishing ground. [C.F. Plourde (1970) and Clark and Munro (1975)].

[3]   This list has expanded dramatically over the intervening 34 years. A particularly fruitful application has been the production and distribution of information, where emphasis shifts to the lack of incentives to provide a good which is subject to common property dissipation. Organizational responses to minimize dissipation include copyright, patent arrangements, and trade secrecy law. Each response reduces dissipation but does not remove it. For instance, the patent right is defined in law, but the right to be the inventor is not. Dissipative competition among potential inventors, similar to the larger and more powerful boats being introduced on the halibut fishery because of quotas, to be the first to invent occurs. (Barzel, 1968, p. 351.)

[4]   This is one of many instances where the same, erroneous in our opinion, representation of the logic of the Coasean analysis is expressed in Farrel (1987). Other examples are:

> ... Third and perhaps most important, people often use decentralization results — especially the Coase theorem — as arguments against government intervention. (p. 116)
> ... perhaps the Coase theorem should be viewed as a second-best result: property-rights (sic) are more efficient than some reasonable alternative. (p. 122)
> This ambiguous result should make us hesitate to use the Coase theorem to argue for *laissez-faire*. (p. 124)

[5]   See the comments on Pigou's enthusiasm for the work of the Interstate Commerce Commission in Coase (1988d pp. 21 and 22).

[6]   Certainly in Canada, empirical studies paint a more mixed picture c.f. Acheson (1985).

[7]   Many economists believe that Coase's reconstruction of Pigou's ar-

guments and remedies fails to reflect the richness of Pigou's work. As Baumol who was sympathetic to many of the insights for analyzing the world with transactions costs provided by Coase stated:

> A simple model shows readily that, property stated, the prescription of the Pigouvian tradition is (at least formally) correct. An appropriately chosen tax, levied only on the factory (without payment of compensation to local residents) is precisely what is needed for optimal resource allocation under pure competition. We will see, however, that the issue Coase himself intended to raise was rather more subtle and his conclusions are not necessarily at variance with the Pigouvian prescription as I interpret it. (1972, P. 309.)

Goldberg has also persuasively argued that Pigou gave as much emphasis to "the difficulties inherent in contractually coordinating the behavior of mortal, imperfect persons" (1981, p. 49.) as to remedial bounties and taxes.

[8] Baumol (1972) argued that if the Pigouvian taxes were properly structured they would achieve an optimum. Coase acknowledged that in 1960 but considered that the best that a Pigouvian tax and subsidy artist could do is make the taxes equal to the direct damages imposed. (For a recent discussion by Coase see 1988d, pp. 179-185.)

[9] J.B. Buchanan (1973).

[10] V. Aivazian and J. Callen (1981) draw attention to this possibility and present an illustrative simple case in which there are gains from global co-operation but there is no core. Although their example assumes no transactions costs between the entities, the entities themselves are firms. Resources would not have clustered into the firms assumed by Aivazian and Callen, if some other configuration would have produced a "game" with a core. Aivazian and Callen do not address this "first round" organizational problem.

In a different vein, Marchand and Russell (1973) argued that Coase's result required separable cost functions. Gifford and Stone (1973) have forcefully argued that Marchand and Russell's criticisms are based on a restricted view of compensation possibilities or of the nature of the damages inflicted.

[11] Mohring and Boyd (1971) argue correctly that the assignment of rights

conditional on occupational choice (for example assigning the right to quiet to doctors) can affect the allocation of rights. In the world described such an assignment would not be made, just as an inferior technology for transforming iron into steel would not be chosen. They relate their comment to Coases's discussion of *Sturges vs. Bridgman.* The point is interesting in the context of this paper, since the conditional right to quiet granted physicians can result in "too many" physicians. The court created "right to quiet" is a common property right and there is no mechanism to prevent the dissipation of its value by physicians entering to share its fruits. A similar issue arises when access to the tax revenue from a scarce resource owned collectively attracts inefficient migration. In a world of transactions costs, more information is required to judge the efficiency of a conditional right.

[12] Why prospective owners would not contract to transfer the right depending on the state is not clear under the assumed conditions. We have arbitrarily ruled that possibility out but return to the point in the subsequent text to argue that it is difficult to conceive how the court could have an advantage in identifying a beneficial deal. The court's advantage may be in avoiding strategic behaviour that deters some beneficial exchanges.

[13] The market solution depends on the courts enforcing promises and exclusivity.

[14] It is worth repeating that the dilemma does not exist in the transactions costless world where the court's decisions in response to shocks would be anticipated by traders. Those who have a chance to receive the resource tomorrow would register their interest in the continuation of economic care of the resource through contingent payments to prospective owners. If income distribution is to have an allocative effect, transactions costs must preclude "insuring" against the decisions of the court.

[15] A curious example of regulation by a court occurs with complex antitrust agreements. An example is the continuing involvement of the United States District Court for the District of Columbia in monitoring the AT&T divestiture decree and determining such details as the lines of business in which the former Bell operating companies will be allowed to participate.

[16] By the creation of new rights we mean the legal definition of the right

that allows an owner to be identified in the courts. Before the shock the costs of such definition are assumed to exceed the gains. For example, the introduction of air conditioners may make the benefit of delineating liability for noise worth the effort.

[17] For example, when redistributing a right to improve allocative efficiency, a court could compensate those who owned the right before. The court would then more clearly replace the market by substituting a result which would have voluntarily been agreed to had there been no transacting costs. Such compensation was not part of the decisions in the cases inspiring Coase's observations. With the introduction of a new right, (c.f. the discussion of property rights in the case of the operation of air conditioners in Demsetz, 1966, p. 66) a compensation scheme would have to encompass all those damaged by the introduction. In most instances, the courts do not attempt to make these compensations and, ironically, play a role analogous to the stereotyped Pigouvian policy maker who balances social costs and benefits from alternative courses of action.

[18] For models incorporating some or all of these different elements see Rubin (1977), Priest (1977), Landes and Posner (1979).

[19] The positive hypothesis that courts do pursue efficiency in their decisions has been examined by Posner, among others. (1977, 1979).

[20] For an insightful interpretation of the American experience see (Allen, 1988).

[21] The monopoly problem is analytically identical to an externalities problem. The expansion of a simple monopolist provides a positive externality to those making inframarginal purchases. Because simple monopolists are not rewarded for generating this benefit, they exclude it from the determination of output. If instead those benefiting paid for the benefit, which amounts to them paying the original prices for inframarginal purchases, the monopolist would expand making a profitable deal for additional trade. Consecutively applied, this becomes perfect discrimination. Perfect discrimination is equivalent to "internalizing" the externality. Alternatively, simple monopoly can be viewed as a common property right problem in which the seller cannot exclude the inframarginal customer from the terms granted to the new customer. That the monopoly problem only exists in a transaction costly world is well known but its consequences are not widely appreciated.

²² For a fishery the domain of exclusivity, dictated by efficiency concerns, depends on the migratory behaviour of fish.

²³ Demsetz (1972) argues that the possibility of extortion in the bargaining between the parties is really a monopoly problem, with the identity of the monopolist being determined by the rights assignment. The monopolist will strip the gains from trade from the other party. This analysis ignores the bilateral nature of the deals being discussed. A possible justification of the court in a transaction costly world is that it reduces dissipation from gaming over the potential surplus in these situations. Samuelson (1967) drew attention to the indeterminacy in bilateral monopoly in discussing Coase's zero transaction cost benchmark.

²⁴ Gordon notes:

> In a few places the fishermen have banded together into a local monopoly, preventing entry and controlling their own operations. By this means, the amount of fishing gear has been greatly reduced and incomes considerably improved. (Gordon, 1954, p. 134.)

See also Campbell (1981) for an account of the involvement by the fishermen's co-operative in the Nova Scotia herring fishery.

²⁵ For example, by not ignoring but examining the reasons why the firm cannot price discriminate among customers, attention is drawn to the second-hand market. If activity in that market cannot be controlled by the firm and the good is durable, the monopolist cannot bar future entry from recycled goods. The recycled materials market will restrict market power, and in many cases make it negligible. (c.f. Bulow, 1982; Coase, 1972; Swan, 1970)

²⁶ We are not arguing that in a transactions cost world there should be no competition policy, but that enlightened policy will be guided by an understanding of transactions costs. For instance, per se prohibitions of a trade practice that can in some circumstances be efficient may still be justified, since the determination of conditions necessary to make distinctions may be too costly to be worthwhile.

²⁷ Despite Knight's heritage, the appearance of Gordon's article in the *Journal of Political Economy* and Coase's residency at Chicago and his editorship of an influential journal emanating from that university, the emerging views on organizations were ambiguously received

in that cathedral of price theory. The prevailing view in the sixties was that the *Journal of Political Economy* published the prestige pieces and the *Journal of Law and Economics* had softer "institutional" material with less scientific content. The insights into institutions provided by transactions costs are cursorily reflected in Friedman's and Stigler's texts on price theory, the definitive texts of Chicago-brand positive economics of the 1950s and 1960s. By the seventies and eighties, this trend began to shift as analytical and mathematical economists became interested in transactions and informational problems. The *Journal of Political Economy* now deals with many of the same issues that have absorbed its "softer" cousin in the past, albeit with more rigour. Nevertheless, that a gap still exists between the two wings of the discipline is evident by what is generally considered to be good price theory at the undergraduate level.

REFERENCES

K. Acheson, "Economic Regulation in Canada: A survey" Ch. 5 in D. McFetridge (ed.) *Canadian Industrial Policy in Action* (University of Toronto Press 1985).

D. Allen, *A Transaction Cost Approach to the Economic Analysis of Marriage* (Ph.D. Thesis, University of Washington, 1988).

V. Aivazian and J. Callen, "The Coase Theorem and the Empty Core" *Journal of Law and Economics*, 24 (April, 1981), pp. 175-181.

Y. Barzel, "Transaction Costs: Are they Just Costs?" *Journal of Institutional and Theoretical Economics (1985)*, pp. 4-16.

Y. Barzel, "The Optimal Timing of Innovations," *Review of Economics and Statistics*, 50 (August, 1968), pp. 348-55.

Y. Barzel and L.A. Kochin, "The Problem of Social Cost and the Transaction Costs-Property Rights Paradigm," *University of Washington Working Paper #86-4*, (February, 1986), pp. 1-23.

W. Baumol, "On Taxation and the Control of Externalities" *American Economic Review* 62 no. 3 (June 1972), pp. 307-322.

J.M. Buchanan and G. Tullock, *The Calculus of Consent: Logical Foundations of Constitutional Democracy* (University of Michigan Press 1962).

J.M. Buchanan, "Coase Theorem and the State" *Natural Resources Journal* 13 (October 1973), pp. 579-594.

J. I. Bulow, "Durable-Goods Monopolists" *Journal of Political Economy* 90 (April, 1982), pp. 314-332.

H.F. Campbell, The Public Regulation of Commercial Fisheries in Canada: The Bay of Fundy Herring Fishery, *Economic Council of Canada Technical Report 20*, Ottawa, 1981.

C. Clark and G.R. Munro, The Economics of Fishing and Modern Capital Theory: A Simplified Approach," *Journal of Environmental Economics and Management* 2 (December 1975), pp. 92-106.

R.H. Coase, "The Nature of the Firm," *Economica*, 4 (November, 1937), pp. 386-405.

R.H. Coase, "The Problem of Social Cost," *Journal of Law and Economics*, 3 (October, 1960), pp. 1-44.

R.H. Coase, "Durability and Monopoly," *Journal of Law and Economics*, 15 (April, 1972), pp. 143-9.

R.H. Coase, "The Nature of the Firm: Origin" *Journal of Law, Economics & Organization* 4, no. 1 (Spring 1988a), pp. 3-18.

R.H. Coase, "The Nature of the Firm: Meaning" *Journal of Law, Economics & Organization* 4, no. 1 (Spring 1988b), pp. 19-32.

R.H. Coase, "The Nature of the Firm: Influence" *Journal of Law, Economics & Organization* 4, no. 1 (Spring 1988c), pp. 33-48.

R.H. Coase, *The Firm, The Market, and the Law* (University of Chicago Press, 1988d).

H. Demsetz, "Some Aspects of Property Rights, *Journal of Law and Economics* IX (October, 1966), pp. 61-70.

H. Demsetz, "Towards a Theory of Property Rights," *American Economic Review* 57 (May, 1967), pp. 347-59.

H. Demsetz, "When Does the Rule of Liability Matter," *Journal of Legal Studies* v. 1, no. 1 (January, 1972), pp. 13-29.

J. Farrell, "Information and the Coase Theorem," *The Journal of Economic Perspectives* v. 1, no. 2 (Fall 1987), pp. 113-130.

A. Gifford Jr. and C. Stone, "Externalities, Liability and the Coase Theorem: a Mathematical Analysis", *Western Economic Journal* (March, 1973), pp. 260-269.

V.P. Goldberg, "Regulation and Administered Contracts," *The Bell Journal of Economics* 7, no. 2 (Autumn 1976), pp. 426-48.

V.P. Goldberg, "Pigou on Complex Contracts and Welfare Economics," *Research in Law and Economics* V. 3 (1981), pp. 39-51.

H.S. Gordon, "The Economic Theory of a Common Property Resource: The Fishery," *Journal of Political Economy*, 62 (1954), pp. 124-142.

J.L. Knetsch, "Some Economic Implications of Matrimonial Property Rules," *University of Toronto Law Journal*, 34 (1984), pp. 263-82.

F.H. Knight, "Some Fallacies in the Interpretation of Social Cost," *The Quarterly Journal of Economics*, 38 (1924), pp. 582-606; reprinted in G.J. Stigler and K.E. Boulding, *A.E.A. Readings in Price Theory* (Chicago: Richard Irwin, 1952).

W.M. Landes and R.A. Posner, "Adjudication as a Private Good" *The Journal of Legal Studies* VII, no. 2 (March 1979) pp. 235-284.

J.R. Marchand and K. Russell, "Externalities, Liability, Separability, and Resource Allocation," *American Economic Review* (September, 1973), pp. 611-620.

J.C. McManus, "An Economic Analysis of Indian Behaviour in the North American Fur Trade," *Journal of Economic History*, 32 (March, 1972), pp. 36-53.

J.C. McManus, "The Costs of Alternative Economic Organizations," *Canadian Journal of Economics* (1975), pp. 335-350.

H. Mohring and J. Boyd, "Analysing "Externalities": "Direct Interaction" vs. "Asset Utilization" Frameworks" *Economica* (1971), pp. 347-361.

C.G. Plourde, "A Simple Model of Replenishable Resource Exploitation," *American Economic Review* 60 (June 1970), pp. 518-521.

R.A. Posner, "Some Uses and Abuses of Economics in Law," *The University of Chicago Law Review* v. 46, no. 2 (Winter 1979), pp. 281-315.

G.L. Priest, "The Common Law Process and the Selection of Efficient Rules," *Journal of Legal Studies* v. VI, no. 1 (January 1977), pp. 65-82.

P.H. Rubin, "Why is the Common Law Efficient?" *Journal of Legal Studies* v. VI, no. 1 (January 1977), pp. 51-64.

P.A. Samuelson, "The monopolistic Competition Revolution," in R. Kuenne (ed.) *Monopolistic Competition Theory: Studies in Impact: Essays in Honor of Edward H. Chamberlin* (Wiley 1967).

P.L. Swan, "The Durability of Goods and Regulation of Monopoly," *Bell Journal* 2 (Spring 1971), pp. 347-357.

O.E. Williamson, "Franchise Bidding for Natural Monopolies — In General and with Respect to CATV," *Bell Journal of Economics* 7 no. 1 (Spring 1976), pp. 73-104.

O.E. Williamson, *The Economic Institutions of Capitalism: Firms, Markets, Relational Contracting* (The Free Press, 1985).

COMMENTS ON THE

ACHESON AND FERRIS PAPER

André Plourde, University of Ottawa,
M.C. Urquhart, Queen's University
and
Douglas W. Allen, Simon Fraser University

ANDRÉ PLOURDE

To someone trained in natural resource economics, the idea of linking transactions costs and common property rights is quite appealing, if for no other reason than both sets of questions draw attention to the nature and consequences of the institutional setting within which exchanges occur. The paper by Acheson and Ferris shows just how fruitful such an approach can be, and their references to Scott Gordon's classic 1954 article reveals the richness of the insights to be gleaned from the literature on common property resources.

If beauty is in the eye of the beholder, then it is doubly true that the meaning of the expression "transactions costs" is in the mind of the user. In addition to offering a formal definition, a recent paper (Allen 1988) discusses a series of different meanings ascribed, either explicitly or implicitly, to this expression by a number of writers on the subject. The approach followed by Acheson and Ferris is not to provide an explicit definition, but rather to describe a situation of zero transactions costs.[1] By implication, situations where at least some of these conditions do not hold (e.g., the generation and dissemination of information is costly, contract design is a costly activity, there are positive enforcement costs) are characterized by positive transactions costs. To a non-specialist like myself, this state of affairs is rather frustrating since it hampers the ability to think formally about these issues while being certain of capturing all of the essential elements of the problem.

One of the results presented by the authors is that: "(t)he costs of arranging transactions make it possible that trade will fail to shift rights to their most highly valued uses." Whatever the definition of transactions costs used, a necessary condition for this result to obtain is that the *nature* of such costs be different from that of the payments to the owners of factors of production encountered in conventional price theory. If this were not the case, then no difference between the auctioneer's solution and that of the social planner would arise as a result of the introduction of transactions costs. Rather, the whole problem would simply be defined away by adding more dimensions over which to optimize, with markets ensuring that the correct marginal conditions are met.

In such a context, the common property problem reminds us that, without the appropriate institutional setting, market forces will not yield an efficient solution. If the rights cannot be costlessly reassigned, then, Acheson and Ferris argue, issues of efficiency and distribution cannot be treated separately. This is a rather important theoretical result, since conventional theory treats efficiency and distribution as dichotomous (the welfare theorems are good examples of this.) If Acheson and Ferris's argument can be applied to the case of lump sum taxes and transfers, then the maximization of social welfare will generally require some trade-off between efficiency and distribution. In other words, cost minimization would now be conditional on the distribution of rights. An earlier message emerges again: privately drawn cost-minimizing contracts could fail to shift rights to their most highly valued uses.

The above implies that, for some initial distributions of rights, a competitive market will not yield a first-best solution (at least, not in the conventional sense of the expression). An excellent section of the paper explores the consequences of and potential remedies to this problem. As with the literature on common property rights, the ensuing discussion focuses on institutional design and the role of courts. Later, the additional insights that the introduction of transaction costs brings to the study of common property resource issues are examined. It appears to me, however, that the analysis would be more complicated were it assumed that the resource had more than one potential use. In such cases, it would not be sufficient to examine the consequences of reallocating the rights to given activities, but comparisons across different uses would be necessary.[2]

In a similar vein, two interrelated points caught my eye. About midway through the paper, the authors toy with the idea that the value of alternative uses could well be state dependent. Toward the end they state: "...the comparison of institutions requires comparison of total benefits rather than just the usual marginal ones." Taken at face value, this raises serious questions about the validity of the marginal analysis that we have all grown to know and love. It also warns the policy analyst that partial equilibrium analysis is much less reliable than might have been thought, and hence that piecemeal policy making is a rather dangerous undertaking. A policy $z1$ in area y might dominate policy $z2$ in the same area when institutional setting $x1$ prevails in related area w. What else have we learned here other than that the economists' usual exhortation in favour of institutional reform may embody more wisdom than previously believed? Not as much as I would have liked. The general equilibrium implications of the existence of transactions costs should, in itself, be the subject of more research.

As the above suggests, these questions force us to think about general equilibrium questions in an entirely different manner. All of a sudden, thinking of an economy — even from a theoretical perspective — as a collection of frictionless markets, which, left to its own devices, will yield an efficient solution just does not do any more: crucial pieces to the puzzle are missing. While the authors argue that such a message was difficult for them "to absorb let alone embrace" their inquiry into the matter is quite convincing to an outside reader.

Allow me to close on a less favourable note. When I read this paper for the first time, I was attending a conference in Quebec City where most participants were sociologists, political scientists, and other species who rather enjoyed a good game of economics-bashing! The keynote speaker made the following argument, which I paraphrase. Economists, he said (dripping with sarcasm), have an interesting concept, that of externalities. His position was clear: "externality" was a synonym for human life. From the textbook example of the upstream polluter and the downstream resident, to the person sitting next to you on the bus who had neglected to use deodorant, all human social activities are examples of externalities. Therefore, if one were to agree with economists that intervention was theoretically warranted whenever an externality is present, then all human social activities should be subject to regulation. His conclusion from this: the notion of externalities as providing a rationale for intervention is vacuous because such a concept is all-encompassing.

A similar type of argument can be made about the role of transactions costs based on the paper by Acheson and Ferris. It may well be that the authors sought primarily to establish the *logical* point that transactions costs matter and may thus provide an efficiency-based rationale for intervention. In itself, this is a worthwhile enterprise and one for which the authors should be commended. Given the existence of transactions costs, what policy makers and justices need, however, are rules that will allow them to separate cases where the potential consequences of such costs are significant and thus where intervention is warranted, from those where market forces are best left unfettered. The paper by Acheson and Ferris offers little guidance on this score.[3] Paradoxically, I think that the reason for this shortcoming is that the authors sought to introduce a theoretical concept and to motivate it by appeals to real-world situations. As a result, the exercise becomes a *description* of a process without any *modelling* of the underlying forces at work. It seems to me that transaction-cost economics will become an even more fruitful field of study when its key ideas are presented in a more formal manner, and thus made more accessible for debate and empirical testing.

NOTES

[1]   The definition provided by Allen (1988), p. 9) seems to be a proper subset of that implicitly given by Acheson and Ferris.

[2]   Some hint of this higher level of complexity is given on pages 43 and 44.

[3]   The authors' discussion of these issues tends toward comparisons of different institutional settings.

REFERENCES

Acheson, Keith and Stephen Ferris (1988) "Origins of Theories of Organization: The Common Property Root," a paper prepared for presentation at the *Festchrift* in Honour of H. Scott Gordon held at Carleton University on November 15, 1988.

Allen, Douglas W. (1988) "What Are Transaction Costs Anyway?" Carleton Industrial Organization Research Unit, Working paper 88-09. Department of Economics, Carleton University, Ottawa.

Gordon, H. Scott (1954) "The Economic Theory of a Common Property Resource: The Fishery," *Journal of Political Economy* 62(1): 124-142.

D23   *Welfare, Property Rights and Economic Policy*

M.C. URQUHART*

I find the Acheson-Ferris paper both interesting and enigmatic. It is especially interesting in that it deals essentially, in my view, with problems of efficiency in an economy arising out of the presence of particular types of externalities in that economy in an extensive and cogent presentation of the main elements of the relevant literature. It is enigmatic in that it appears to accept the judgment of Ronald Coase and some of his followers that traditional economics has been gravely deficient in its analysis of how an economic system works and of the implications therefrom for public policy, because it has ignored "transactions costs."[1]

The externalities to which I refer, I classify, for my convenience, into two types, the first associated with the common property problems that Scott Gordon addressed in the article (1954) discussed by Acheson-Ferris and the second associated with the matters that Ronald Coase addressed in his "The Problem of Social Cost" (1960). The first category involves the external effects that are the result of the summing up of the consequences of the economic actions of individual decision makers, in response to prices in markets, in cases where the participants are not aware of the externality: such I believe, are the externalities of the actions of small fishermen as atomistic decision makers in the use of a "free" common property resource. Second, there are the externalities that occur when the actions of one decision maker impinge, outside the market system, in definite and identifiable ways directly on the well-being of other decision makers in such fashion that the decision makers involved are aware of the consequences of the externality: such I believe, are all of the cases of the 1960 Coase article in which Coase begins "This paper is concerned with those actions of business firms which have harmful effects on others." As Acheson-Ferris show, there had been quite limited prior discussion of the common property resource. On the other hand, there had been much discussion of the Coase type externalities (see Pigou) with which Coase disagreed.

---

*   It is a real pleasure for me to participate in a symposium in recognition of the work of Scott Gordon. And it is an especial pleasure to comment on a paper which gives recognition to Scott Gordon's seminal contribution to the common property problem in economics.

In order to economize on space and words I deal with allegations about the shortcomings of traditional economics immediately, since one's view on this matter provides background to the analysis of the economies of both sorts. In my view, the alleged shortcomings of traditional analysis for dealing with policy questions related to externalities have been greatly overstated by Coase and his followers and it appears to me that Acheson-Ferris have gone some way in adopting this overstatement.

The Acheson-Ferris (and Coase) characterization of traditional economics does not correspond to such economics as I have known it. Acheson-Ferris begin with the statement that "economic models typically focus on the equilibrium consumption and production flows of a frictionless world" and, a few sentences later, "No resources are allocated to making the firms and markets function." In Coase's description of such a view of the economy there are no "transaction costs." The Coasian world without transactions costs (in his view, the world of traditional economics) comprises an economic organization in which "the price system is assumed to work without cost" (See quotation in Acheson-Ferris). This presumably means that there are no costs involved in making agreements about transfer among decision-making units of rights to economically significant entities and enforcement thereof.[2] It is an economy of completeness of relevant knowledge and of complete certainty. There is not even a need for firms in the co-ordination of factor services in production. However, the argument goes, once any cost of transactions (in the Coasian sense) is present then the nature of the economy and the way of handling externalities in it may change: on one hand, firms now are formed to avoid or at least minimize transactions costs by internalizing many transactions within the firm; on the other hand, some transactions among firms may not be undertaken since the costs exceed the benefit. Traditional economics has not taken account of these transactions costs.

The foregoing description of the content of conventional (or traditional) economics may fit some of the expositions of the Walrasian general equilibrium but is certainly not representative of traditional economics in general. The latter must involve some abstraction but it is much more relevant to the real world than Coase implies. A central feature of traditional economics is an explanation of how an economic system based on specialization and decentralized decision making operates to bring about order rather than chaos in a world where life is ongoing, where there is not complete knowledge on the part of all decision makers about the present, much less the future, but where, nevertheless, economic decision and economic action must take place. And while much economics is elaborated in terms of static equilibria, that means only an equilibrium of today based on today's knowledge and judgments; tomorrow may not be like today, partly because it is planned that way and partly because the circumstances of the future are different than expected.

It is axiomatic that economic action takes place only as a result of decisions of individual decision-making units. Among decision-making units are the firms which are responsible for the co-ordination of factor inputs to produce commodity or service outputs: their existence is explained by the complexities of production and the need for taking action in addition to that of the other decision makers, the consumers and owners of factors of production, in ever changing circumstances. Except in a world of unbroken repetitious routine, it is pure fancy to think of production, which involves elaborate conjuncture of use of inputs, choice of technology and selection of outputs, in the absence of a firm decision maker. And contrary to the allegations of Coase and followers, there has been a good deal of discussion of the role and nature of the firm: Marshall wrote at length about it; Knight, Viner and many others did likewise. Discussion of economies and diseconomies of scale, involving among other things indivisibilities, have for long involved considerations of optimum firm size and more recently, literature relative to the firm has been large, indeed. Of course there are costs of co-ordination. But these are part of the production process and are to be minimized just as are other costs. And it has been realized that one goes outside the firm to achieve the benefits of specialization when the creation of separate firms becomes the most efficient way of achieving the advantages of specialization in production.

It does not follow from the foregoing view that an approach that uses a concept of transactions costs is valueless. It may be an alternative to conventional analysis for some purposes and may be particularly useful in some cases. But it also does not follow that the application of the concept of transactions costs is essential for dealing with all or most issues of efficiency in the economy. For example, an explanation of inefficiency of monopoly on the basis of transactions costs of price discrimination by the monopolist being so high as to make the monopolist forego such price discrimination adds nothing to conventional analysis and indeed may obscure issues of public policy with regard to price discrimination and who should benefit from surpluses; nor do transactions costs help in the explanation of the working of that large part of the economy that is not subject to externalities in the Coasian sense. It is because the concept of transactions costs was not nearly as revolutionary for dealing with policy issues related to efficiency as Coase seemed to think, that it has not assumed a big role in traditional economics. And this consequence is not because economists have not understood Coase's arguments.

I wish now to say a few words about the common property externality question and Coase-type externality in that order. The realization of the fact that "the" common property resource problem arises out of assignment of property rights was most fruitful. It is true that there were antecedents dealing with the role of property rights in somewhat similar situations but the examples had tended to be contrived. Scott Gordon's paper dealt with real circumstances of an important industry, the fisheries; and the applicability of his analysis to the utilization of petroleum and gas resources, pollution of a common "free" water supply, and the like, was obvious. In addition, as Acheson and Ferris point out, it supplied, among other things, information of what not to do to improve matters as well as having great value in deciding what to do. Finally, as well as being clearly written, Scott Gordon's article was written with good taste which did not involve belting someone over the head first, to show how stupid predecessors had been. His analysis was immediately adopted by traditional economics. Acheson-Ferris present the matter admirably and I have no further comment.

I come now to the Coase contribution in his 1960 article and I want to restrict my comments to the following three points of his argument. First, and most explicitly, he demonstrates that if a harmful externality from the actions of one economic unit damages (lowers the net product of) another economic unit directly (imposes an external cost), the best "corrective" action for social efficiency is not necessarily to make the offending party eliminate the externality completely or perhaps, even, at all. From a social point of view, the extra product arising from the action which caused the external "harm" may be greater than the loss of product suffered by the recipient of the "harm." In this case, other things being equal, the socially optimum level of harm, from an efficiency perspective, will be at the point where the marginal gain to the offender from being able to inflict the harm just matches the marginal loss to the recipient of the harm. It is worth mentioning, aside from Coase's writings, that these situations, where economic units directly affect the well-being of other economic units, observedly, and where there is a gain if some elements of these externalities continue to exist, are widely characteristic of urban conurbations where it is socially optimum that they continue to exist. This circumstance of cities and towns was implicitly understood before Coase, but his formal statement of the matter was a valuable contribution. And he cited many legal judgments in Britain that give recognition to this phenomenon.

Second, Coase demonstrated that, in such a case, given private property rights, the ability to make contracts, costlessly, and the ability to transfer money *costlessly* from one party to the other, it does not matter which party is made liable for the harmful effects because the two parties together will make a deal that leads to the largest joint (social) value product: the assignment of liability just determines which party pays the other to adopt the scale of output that is socially optimal and individually most beneficial to each party given what the legal provisions are. In such circumstances, the private sector will yield an optimal allocation of resources to achieve efficiency, regardless of the liability assignments.

Third, Coase admits that if there are costs of making contracts and transferring money (transactions costs in his terminology), the situation alters: the assignment of liability to one private party rather than the other can affect the level of the social product achieved in the private bargaining, a point that he expounded in his 1960 article and that he illustrated by an arithmetic example in his 1988 book. In addition, the costs of contracting and exchanging money may be so great that costs of private contracting, especially if substantial numbers of decision-making units are involved, exceed the benefits that would derive from private agreement on limiting the "harmful" externality, in which case, an alternative that may be less costly is government regulation, though he is less than sanguine about the quality of much of the public regulation.

So far so good. Coase's social cost article explained and clarified some aspects of how harmful externalities may affect the working of an economy. It undoubtedly made a significant contribution to an understanding of the reciprocal nature of external effects. I should add that there had been prior recognition that there may be costs of eliminating the undesirable externalities that exceed the external damage and so are not justified: Pigou makes this point explicitly. I wish just to express two reservations about the Coase arguments on their own grounds.

The first reservation may be niggling but I believe it has some relevance. Coase appears to ignore the fact that direct bargaining among individuals does not necessarily lead to a socially optimum efficiency solution: the arguments of game theory, the free rider problem and the like illustrate the efficiency problems of such negotiation. Our knowledge of the parameters of these effects is very limited, but so is Coase's.

The second reservation relates to the extent to which private contracting is relevant to the Coase type problem quite apart from Coase's own reservations related to his "transactions costs." Let me begin with a specific case which is directly relevant to the Coase argument. In the early days of settlement of the Canadian prairies' park belt, there were both grain farmers and cattle raisers (Coase's term). It was clear that free access of even one cattlebeast to cropland would do such damage that the gains to the cattle raiser would be much less than the loss to the typical grain farmer; the socially efficient optimum (if exclusion was economically manageable) was no cattle on the cropland. It was also clear that the least costly way of keeping the cattle off the cropland was to build cattle-proof (barbed wire) fences and that the social efficiency gains from having the barbed wire were at least enough to pay for all costs.

This situation was, in fact, that of the part of Alberta that I knew in the early days. At that time there was much unoccupied land, school land, Hudson Bay land, C.P.R. land, road allowance land and even homestead land that was just there and the owners did not try to make any commercial use of it. The law permitted cattle to run freely; it also permitted barbed wire fences. Since the grain farmers' gains from exclusion of cattle in general much exceeded the cattle raisers' loss plus the cost of fencing (an empirical assertion on my part), the grain farmers did the fencing — the cattle raisers had no incentive to contribute to costs of fencing.[3] There was still an efficiency issue from the social point of view. Was the exclusion of cattle from farmland achieved at least cost by fencing the cropland or by fencing the cattle raisers' land? In the early days, before much of the land had been put under crop, fencing the cropland was undoubtedly the least costly; from a social point of view, that matter probably had something to do with the legal arrangements of the early days. As time passed, as more land was put under crop (much of it previously unoccupied) and less land was used for cattle raising, the time came when it was undoubtedly less expensive from a social point of view to fence the cattle land and not the cropland. In fact, as time passed, the law was changed and cattle raisers were required by law to keep their cattle off other farmers' land: they were required to build the fences.

Now, in the abstract, the crop farmers could conceivably have made a bargain with the cattle raisers, once it was socially cheaper to fence cattle land jointly, to pay for the fences around the cattle land rather than the farmland. However, such action would not have been feasible, given the large numbers that would have been involved in the agreements, the problems of delineation of boundaries of negotiation, the free-rider problem and the like (prohibitive transaction costs if one wishes to look at it that way.) There is indeed a further twist to this bargaining problem. As long as cattle raisers could let their cattle run freely and crop farmers must put up the fences there would be some land which has a higher net product from crop growing than ranching but not sufficiently high to pay for a fence. Once the cattle land is fenced this marginal land should not be fenced for cattle raising, but should be transferred to crop growing. If the cattle raiser has to pay for the fence the land will not be fenced for cattle raising and will be left for its highest productivity use.

There is little in the way of bargaining here and I expect that the situation described above has many counterparts in other situations. In particular, probably the most extensive existence of the Coase type externalities appear in urban conurbations. That both harmful and beneficial externalities abound here is clear. And that the best solution does not involve elimination, *per se*, of all harmful effects is evident. It is also clear (or, at least, appears to be clear, on the basis of behaviour of centuries) that the optimum arrangements in urban centres cannot be entirely solved by bargains among contending decision makers — it would be unmanageably complex — although the issues involved here cannot be resolved without bringing into consideration the provision of public goods.[4] The nature of the alternatives, their effectiveness and their costs, then become major issues. My only comment is that I find it difficult to believe that an approach centring on considerations of transactions costs will be nearly as fruitful as Acheson and Ferris appear to believe.

NOTES

[1]   The Coase script on which I base my comments is all found in R.H. Coase, *The Firm, the Market and the Law* (University of Chicago Press, 1988) which contains, in addition to reprints of his most relevant articles, two new parts, an introductory essay on "The Firm, the Market and the Law" (31 pages) and "Notes of Problems of Social Costs" (29 pages).

[2]   I have not found a concise definition of transaction costs in my reading of Coase's work: Do they include costs of transferring resources as well as costs of making contracts? Are these once and for all costs (capital costs) or are they recurring? If they are a capital cost they are like any other capital cost. I must add that, in the literature, the term is sometimes used in a tautological manner.

[3]   The cattle raisers would have fenced land only if cattle raising had a higher net product than crop farming even though the latter was sufficiently high to pay for the fence.

[4]   I have not commented on Coase's discussions of the inefficiencies of public action to resolve such problems. That is another matter.

DOUGLAS W. ALLEN*   D23

A FISH OUT OF WATER:
A FALLACY IN THE APPLICATION OF COMMON PROPERTY

INTRODUCTION

In his seminal 1954 work, H. Scott Gordon argued that in a resource like the fishery, where free access to fish seemed an unavoidable fact of life, the value of the fishery is completely dissipated as fishermen enter the industry until the value of their average product is equal to their alternative wage. The source of Gordon's result is the common property aspect of the fishery — no one owns the fishery. In the spirit of Marshall's dictum for economic theory "The Many in the One, the One in the Many," economists have applied Gordon's analysis to many aspects of the world around us. The efforts of this paper are directed towards a particular branch of applications — those where the analysis of common property is quite inappropriate, since the absent property right is actually held by someone.

In all of the examples below, individuals or firms under the control of individuals are treated as a common property resource. In the case of retailing, for example, customers are treated as passive fish inadvertently caught by the retailer who casts the broadest net. In these examples, as in the original Gordon piece, ownership or property rights are treated in an all-or-nothing sense. In the fishery, fish are completely unowned and free for the taking, while the fisherman's boat, equipment, and caught fish are his sole possessions. For the major point of this paper I maintain this distinction. When property rights are delineated, I mean completely; that is, there is perfect exclusion and transferability over the owned good. Thus, maintaining the assumptions used in these applications, I demonstrate a common fallacy among them.

---

*   I would like to apologize to Dr. Seuss for borrowing one of his titles, and I thank anyone who would bear responsibility for such a fishy piece.

SOME FISHY APPLICATIONS

FISHING AND RETAILING

When a fisherman increases his efforts he thins out the uncaught stock of fish, imposes a negative externality on his competitors, and contributes to overfishing. Along the same lines, when a retailer increases his selling efforts, it reduces the uncaught stock of customers, and thereby reduces the productivity of other retailers. Can we conclude, by analogy, that there is over-retailing? Goldberg (1986) says yes we can. He argues that retailers overinvest in their effort to "capture" buyers to the point where all gains attributable to selling are dissipated. He states:

> Real resources will be used to convert people from potential customers (live fish) into actual customers (dead, or at least captured, fish). The customer is of no value to the seller until he is captured. The selling effort of each firm will raise the costs of its competitors, and, if the firms fail to take this into account, they will collectively overspend on selling. (pp. 173-74, 1976)

I intend to argue that Goldberg's case can only be made by treating consumers *exactly* as if they were fish, and that allowing for consumer's freedom to choose reveals a common error in the application of common property.

There is a crucial difference between Gordon's fishery and Goldberg's pool of customers — unlike fish, consumers are made better off by an increased "harvest." In understanding why, we come to the heart of what is at issue here. An exchange is a voluntary action, and both parties must perceive the trade as making them no worse off. When a buyer becomes the customer of a particular outlet he is not "captured," rather he has exercised his right to buy; the existence of this right is what makes him a buyer. Since the consumer decides which retailer will "capture" him, he must be made better off.[1] Fish are forced from the seas and therein lies the difference.[2] An example may help.

Diagram 1 below shows the market supply and demand curves in some retailing market.[3] There are n retailers with initial constant marginal costs of $6 ($S_1$) and n consumers with marginal values (D_1) of $6 for the current output level Q'. Suppose with no selling effort each retailer has a $1/n$ share in sales at a price of $6, and therefore earns zero rent. Increases in one retailer's selling effort increases that retailer's share at the expense of the others. However, as mentioned, selling effort must be valued by the consumers because exchanges are voluntary, thus marginal values must increase as well. If the effort by the seller is valued more by the consumer than its cost, both firms and consumers are better off by the selling effort, and we have a new equilibrium. The curve *ee* is a locus of equilibrium points for various levels of quality. As diagram 1 shows, the process stops at A, with an equilibrium price of $P*$ and quantity of $Q*$ traded. Hence competition among retailers does increase selling effort (hence costs), but it also increases the value of what is being traded. Rent is not dissipated, rather it is created and (at least in this example) transferred to consumers. The analogy between fishing and selling centres on the pool of consumers being unowned, but it is only unowned with respect to retailers — *consumers are not common property*. They own the right to decide whether to buy or not, and this cannot be ignored. Holding consumer behaviour exogenous is tantamount to allowing fish bargaining rights with their predators.[4]

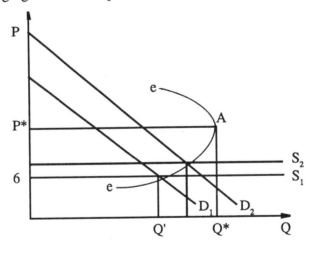

Diagram 1

FISHING AND THE MARKET

In a paper that predates Goldberg by two years, Copes argues that all competitive markets exhibit the open access attribute of the fishery and that generally all market rents are dissipated. Copes uses an example of a gasoline station market to make his point.

> In the gasoline retailing case, the 'commons' is the market
> which service stations may use free of charge in order to make
> tankfill (sic) sales. ... Just as fishermen are unconstrained in
> taking fish away from one another, because there is no re-
> source user cost, so service station operators are unconstrained
> in taking tankfill sales away from one another because there
> is no market user cost. With no limit on the number of serv-
> ice stations that may enter the market, additional stations will
> be attracted until average returns drop to the level where there
> are no net benefits over and above normal returns to be earned.
> (p. 54, 1984)

Copes assumes that consumers are indifferent towards the density of
service stations, which technically allows him to carry over the common
property analysis. Assuming consumers do not care about the density of
retail stations may be the same as assuming fish do not care who their
captor is, but it is certainly false. Therefore, Copes' conclusion that "Just
as a fish stock is economically overfished under open entry conditions,
so a market is economically overused under such conditions" is entirely
irrelevant. Consumers value closer gas stations, and when this is accounted
for under the conditions of Diagram 1 it is not the rent that dissipates but
the problem.

An early, and better, analysis of the market as a commons is by Carroll,
et al, (1979). These authors recognized the tension between the notion of
perfect competition and the perfect competitor. Every seller would like
to see entry into his market closed to all others, yet the nature of competition is to have open entry. In their words:

> Competition works because the new entrants to a market re-
> duce the price of the commodity being sold by established
> firms. Since the "cost" of such a revenue loss is borne by
> firms collectively, new firms take no account of the effect of
> revenue reduction upon existing firms. The motive force of a
> competitive market is actually the uncompensated external-
> ity. (p. 608, 1979)

To drive home the point one more time, the market may be open to
competitors, but the gains from trade are not up for grabs — consumers
do not bite at the first price that comes their way.

THE DELAWARE PROBLEM

Ignoring the actual allocation of ownership before, during, and after an
exchange leads to rather backwards policy positions. As a case in point,

consider Professor Cary's 1974 attack on Delaware's liberal corporation law. Although neither he nor his critics use the common property fishing analogy, the fallacy of his analysis is a failure to recognize that property rights do exist.

As is well known, Delaware, since the beginning of this century, has led the way in liberal corporate legislation. This legislation, which has resulted in approximately 40 percent of corporate charters created in Delaware, creates a more profitable environment for firms to incorporate under. Cary and others, however, have argued that it has led to a "race to the bottom" (read dissipation). As with fishing, Delaware's actions have led to too much competition. Cary states, "Indeed, the whole process is contagious. Other states understandably want to encourage companies to remain at home and therefore try to emulate Delaware by revising their acts along similar lines." According to Delaware's critics, when corporations swim around in the public pool, effort by the various states to catch them and bring them home for dinner is viewed as dissipating the gains from the corporate fishery.

As in the case of retailing, corporations own the right to decide their state of residence. Competition for domicile can only benefit both parties, with the terms of trade merely deciding the allocation of the gains from trade. When all rights are owned, and an exchange is voluntary, neither party has an incentive to dissipate anything. The situation with Delaware is really a race to the top.[5]

WHEN DO FISH LIVE OUT OF WATER?

By now it should be very apparent that I have merely been arguing the case that Coase made almost 30 years ago — when property rights are perfectly defined, there is no social cost. I am not arguing that there is no such thing as common property, however — only that it may not be so common. Many resources exist in the public domain and are accessible to any who want them, but in these cases there are rights that are unowned. Consider Diagram 1 again, where both curves shifted vertically parallel. Leffler (1982) has shown that when these curves do not shift in this fashion, then Q^* will not maximize the gains from trade and nor will consumers and producers necessarily agree on what the optimum quality and quantity is. This result occurs because intramarginal units are not taken into account by the price mechanism. In terms of this analysis, there is a common property problem because the right to surplus on intramarginal units is poorly defined by an allocation mechanism based on marginal values and marginal costs.

To use one more example, consider the state's ability to approve patents and issue them first come, first served. Is the value of the discovery not dissipated?[6] In this stylized example it would be, however, only because the government owns nothing of value — namely the invention. Patents are useless without an invention, and inventions lie in the public domain, not patents. Common property problems exist because effort by inventors can capture a return owned by no one.

CONCLUSION

My point, although by now an obvious one, is that before the application of common property can be applied there must be a common property problem. This point is not without policy implications. Goldberg, for example, claims that in an effort to reduce the selling externality retailers may use exclusive territories, place voluntary restrictions on placement and size of signs, store hours, and the ability to "hard sell." However, if the argument of this paper is correct and consumers do not sit idly by in the public domain, then these actions by retailers can be easily interpreted as naked restraints of trade.[7] When all rights are completely owned the retailers are earning zero economic profits — a result economists are usually quite comfortable with. Under these conditions what is being dissipated in the retailing case (as far as the sellers are concerned) is a monopoly rent.

It is more likely the case that such self-imposed constraints do result from common property, but on margins other than the one examined by Goldberg.[8] It is the task of the economist to find the true common property nature of retailing, markets, and government behaviour. There is no gain in creating an imaginary problem by ignoring the ownership rights of the consumer. Merely drawing on the colourful fishing analogy, if you'll pardon the pun, simply creates a red herring.

NOTES

1   Consumers are no more captured than the seller. Indeed, there is a reciprocal nature to Goldberg's argument; that is, consumers do too much shopping as they compete for goods from sellers who are in the public domain. Thus if Goldberg's application of common property is extended to its logical conclusion, we have too much selling, and too much buying — trade is a bad thing.

2   Thomas and Bean (1974) use the analogy of too much fishing in estimating slave trade profits. It seems plausible that slaves, like fish, must be captured under duress.

3   These curves are drawn under the condition that the curves shift vertically parallel, and I do this to concentrate on the issue at hand. Later I mention the ramifications of allowing for different types of shifts.

4   To be fair to Goldberg, he does say the following: "The choice and search effort of consumers is suppressed in order to explore the implications of selling activity by manufacturers and retailers." This, however, is like the man who looks for his keys under the street light, not because he lost them there, but because the light is better. By ignoring the value customers place on selling effort Goldberg states:

>   Unlike the fishing context, however, the burden of adaptation does not fall entirely on the sellers. The customers can adapt as well. ... They can shop intelligently, travel to suppliers who engage in little selling effort, and so forth. ... An individual can avert his eyes from a billboard... (p. 176, 1976)

5   See Winter (1977) and Fishel (1982) for more detailed legal criticisms of Cary (1974).

6   Ignoring any other institutional features designed to prevent such a thing.

7   Carroll *et. al.*, recognize that efforts to create rents on the part of firms comes at the expense of consumers under the conditions discussed here.

8   See Ferris (1988) for an alternative explanation of restricted store hours, for example.

REFERENCES

Carroll, Ciscil, and Chisholm, "The Market as a Commons: An Unconventional View of Property Rights," *Journal of Economic Issues*, Vol. XIII, no 2, June 1979

W.L. Cary, "Federalism and Corporate Law: Reflections Upon Delaware," *Yale Law Journal*, Vol. 83, no. 4, March 1974

P. Copes, "The Market as an Open Access Commons: A Neglected Aspect of Excess Capacity," *De Economist*, 132, no. 1, 1984

J.S. Ferris, "Time, Space and Shopping: The Regulation of Shopping Hours," Carleton Industrial Organization Research Unit, Working Paper 88-06

D.R. Fischel, "The 'Race to the Bottom' Revisited: Reflections on Recent Developments in Delaware's Corporation Law," *Northwestern University Law Review*, Vol. 76, no. 6, 1982

V. Goldberg, "Fishing and Selling," *The Journal of Legal Studies*, Vol. 15, January 1986

K. Leffler, "Ambiguous Changes In Product Quality," *American Economic Review* Vol. 72, no. 5, 1982

R.A. Posner, *Antitrust Law: An Economic Perspective* (The University of Chicago Press, 1976)

Thomas and Bean, "The Fishers of Men: The Profits of the Slave Trade," *The Journal of Economic History* December 1974

G. Tullock, "The Welfare Costs of Tariffs, Monopolies, and Theft," *The Western Economic Journal* 1968

R.K. Winter, Jr., "State Law, Shareholder Protection, and the Theory of the Corporation," *Journal of Legal Studies*, Vol. 6, no. 2, June 1977

Chapter IV

LUNCHEON REMARKS:
A TRIBUTE TO SCOTT GORDON

David Farr, Carleton University
and
Stephen Kaliski, Queen's University

DAVID FARR

Scott Gordon was a formative figure in the early years of Carleton University. He joined the faculty in 1948, when the six-year-old institution was still Carleton College. The full-time student enrolment was under 600; there were perhaps 20 full-time faculty members. The College consisted of one building, a red-brick Spanish-style structure in the Glebe district which had been built around 1914 for the Ottawa Ladies College. Because we were a small institution and because we all worked together in a confined space, collegiality was our watchword. In a tiny office on the second floor were two historians, later three; next door a somewhat larger room held one, then two economists, two then three political scientists and later, a sociologist. Across the hall were modern languages and mathematics; upstairs were philosophy, English, journalism and engineering. We had a room furnished with a handsome oak table with carved legs, which some said had once been a harpsichord case, where we held faculty meetings. We also ate our lunches from brown bags and some of us dozed there before the 2 p.m. classes. In this environment, where we were constantly talking with our colleagues from other disciplines, there was plenty of opportunity for one individual to leaven the mass. This is the role which I feel Scott played in the infant Carleton College. As a colleague Scott was always stimulating, full of insights about his subject and its relationship to other areas of knowledge, concerned with the way the University was being governed and should be governed. Additionally, he always had the courage of his convictions and the ability to express his views clearly and forcefully. He was an intellectual leader in our little community.

I am one of several who are paying tribute to Scott Gordon and the Economics Department on this happy occasion. To avoid possible overlapping, I have decided to describe, in general terms, Scott's participation in Carleton's academic affairs. I do this from the standpoint of one who was a colleague of Scott's during his whole period at Carleton, 1948-1966. I would like to touch on Scott's role in three areas of university life.

The first, and basic area, is curriculum. Scott believed passionately (I am sure he still does) in the value of a broadly-based liberal education, one that brought out the relationship between disciplines. He was an early advocate of the interdisciplinary approach, although I don't think we used the term as glibly 40 years ago. He was one of the architects of Carleton's common first year curriculum in Arts: English, a language other than English, a science or mathematics, a social science and philosophy. We felt it was a good introduction to the more specialized study of the upper years. I think the common first year survived during Scott's years at Carleton but it was eventually overwhelmed by the attacks of the departments, each wanting its own preparation for its students. Supplementing this approach, Scott joined the group who believed that it was important that students in the social sciences and history read something significant during the summer following their first year. The object was to introduce them to the various social sciences in which they were to major. They were given an oral examination in September on what they had read. Scott helped to choose the titles for the summer reading list and took his place faithfully in the long and tedious conversations in which we probed the students on their intellectual journeyings. It was a noble experiment but, like the common first year, it did not survive in the compartmentalized academic atmosphere that was shortly to prevail.

Scott also paid attention to the faculty in his campaign for a broad interdisciplinary approach to research and teaching. He was one of the founders of the Social Sciences Society, a monthly discussion group that met at faculty members' homes to hear and discuss papers. Now we would call it a colloquium. We have many today but none on a faculty-wide basis. He took up enthusiastically (although the idea came from someone else) the project of a spring conference of faculty members and administrators to discuss problems and prospects in university education. It was a sort of academic retreat held in a country setting shortly after the end of the winter term. After almost 40 years, the Carleton spring conference survives. It still bears testimony to Scott Gordon's vision of the university as a community of teachers and researchers talking together, not a congeries of self-preoccupied departments.

Finally, in the area of curriculum, there was Scott Gordon the chairman of the committee on commerce. If you read through old Faculty Board minutes at Carleton, this is how Scott's name most frequently appears: chairman of the commerce committee. I suspect that secretly Scott did not care much for the School of Commerce, as it was then called. When he discovered that it was to be established at Carleton he made sure that it became an adjunct of the economics department. A member of the economics department was always head of the school, at least in the first decade or more, and the economics department formulated the curriculum for commerce. Scott was continually troubled by the suspicion that too much accounting was creeping into the commerce curriculum. He was also convinced that commerce students often did their utmost to avoid economics courses. He kept them rigidly to the economics requirement, not from a defensive stance but because he believed that the rigour of this subject was good for aspiring business people. I suspect he still does.

Another aspect of university life in which Scott was heavily involved was in promoting faculty participation in the government of the university. I can't remember him making parallel claims for students, but this is the fifties I am recalling, not the sixties. He was a leading spirit in a faculty committee elected in 1955 to consult with the board of governors on the selection of a new president. The board chose Claude Bissell; I don't know if it was influenced by the committee's listing of qualities it considered desirable for the next president of Carleton. Ironically, the chairman of the board in 1955 was James Coyne, with whom Scott had more than a little to do five or six years later! Scott was also a member of a key committee appointed to draw up a scheme for the faculty review of the president's recommendations for promotion. Its report proposed that the faculty should not only review, but should have the right to present promotion recommendations of its own. The committee's work led directly to the present machinery at Carleton: a Senate committee on promotions.

Then there was the question of forming an academic staff association to keep the administration aware of the trend of salaries at other universities and outside the universities. To some the formation of a staff association was a radical venture, an invitation to academic terrorism. I remember how, invoking the contemporary struggle for independence in

Kenya, we called our organization the "Mau Mau." I have been looking at the one-page minutes of the first meeting of the "Mau Mau," November 18 1952. There were 26 individuals (almost the entire full-time faculty) present. Scott, with his keen sense of the practical, moved that the annual membership fee be set at 50 cents but that we should also ask the administration to supply secretarial assistance and stationery! His motion was passed unanimously and 50 cents a year became the levy for the "Mau Mau." It was Scott who pointed out in the mid fifties that a great change was on the horizon for university funding with the appearance of the federal government's grants. This would bring more largesse and flexibility into university salaries. The Carleton "Mau Mau," he argued, should not be backward in pressing its case. We did, although some of us did not see much chance of having it accepted. But it was, to a large extent, and the revolution (if I can call it that) in the escalation of university salary levels in Canada began in the mid-fifties. I give Scott Gordon credit for seeing the long-term trends in public support for higher education in Canada and having the confidence to speak out on the subject. Later, in 1960-61, Scott served as president of a staff association which had outgrown its "Mau Mau" beginnings.

The last of Scott's contributions to Carleton which I wish to mention was his insistence that university people have a duty to comment openly on public issues. They must, however, be well prepared. Universities as critics had not been present in the Canadian tradition. Certain academics, such as Frank Underhill, King Gordon and F.R. Scott, had carried out a running criticism of economic and social policies during the thirties. But I think it was Scott's attack on the monetary policies of the Bank of Canada, embodied in the popular pamphlet, *The Economists versus the Bank of Canada* (1961) that marked the first time a group of academic persons had come together to criticize, not from an ideological viewpoint, a specific policy decision of government. I don't think I am wrong in giving the encounter this significance. In taking up the cudgels against James Coyne and the board of the Bank of Canada, Scott Gordon put a small liberal arts college, just growing into a university, prominently before the Canadian public. Now, 30 years later, at a time when academic people have become apologists or critics of every decision of government, I salute the forthright stand which Scott and his colleagues took over the policies of the Bank of Canada. They were well-briefed, they were moderate and fair in the exposition of their views. Their work still serves as a model for academic critiques of government policy.

I want to conclude with two anecdotes concerning Scott as a colleague. I don't know what they illustrate, except the nature of the man. Scott always impressed me as being "plugged in," as they say, to the outside world. He might teach in a small college but he knew his way around, downtown in the federal government, away at universities in Montreal, Toronto or New York. In Ottawa he maintained these links by the telephone. Simple, you say, how else? But in those distant days the universities (certainly Carleton) did not feel an obligation to provide faculty members with a personal phone. If you wanted one, you paid for it yourself. Scott was the first of the junior faculty members at Carleton to acquire a telephone. Soon we were all using it. The situation became highly inconvenient. Scott arranged for a hutch to be cut in the wall between the office of economics and political science and the history office next door. By this means the telephone could be passed back and forth between the offices. I can't remember whether we ever helped Scott with his telephone bill. It is characteristic of him that he never asked us.

A second anecdote dates from 1969, when Scott was invited to deliver the Plaunt Lectures, Carleton's premier lecture series. He spoke on the subject, "Social Science and the Modern Man." The first of his two lectures was scheduled for Thursday, February 27, a bright cold day. A group of us waited in the room behind the stage in the Alumni Theatre for Scott and Barbara, who were flying up from Indiana in Scott's airplane. It grew close to 8.30 p.m. and there was no Scott. Mr. Dunton, our president, thrust Scott's lecture, which had luckily been sent in advance, into my hands. "Here," he said, "you'd better be prepared to read this if Scott doesn't arrive." I began hurriedly skimming the pages, convinced of the hopelessness of my ever giving Scott's emphasis to the text. A few minutes later, just as Mr. Dunton was about to go on stage to tell the audience that the lecturer would not be present, Scott and Barbara appeared at the door at the back of the hall. They had run into rough weather or engine trouble at Toronto, had put down but had been able to catch a commercial flight to Ottawa at the last moment. I don't know what this story demonstrates, except perhaps Scott's resourcefulness, but I know that I was never as glad in my life to see someone as I was to see Scott Gordon that night!

For all of us, it is good to see Scott Gordon again. Thank you, Scott, for enriching our little community at Carleton during those early days. May you continue to enliven a wider university world, here and in the United States, for many years to come.

STEPHEN KALISKI

It is as much a pleasure and a privilege to participate in this celebration of Scott Gordon and his ongoing work as it is to have been a colleague of his, first here at Carleton and then at Queen's. I hope that I have dipped into Scott's work sufficiently to have formed some appreciation of its scope and depth. While our interests overlap, however, particularly in that we have long shared a concern about macroeconomic policy, I clearly cannot claim any qualifications to give you an assessment of the body of his work. Indeed, as the variety of the papers offered on this occasion testifies, there are probably few economists who have worked on a broad enough canvas to do so.

Let me then turn to the more realistic task of trying to summarize a few large themes that I personally think I have learnt from Scott's work or had reinforced by it. He and you will have to judge whether they bear any resemblance to what he may have intended to teach.

First of all, there is the important notion that economics, as well as being an important and unified body of analysis, the development of which is well worth studying, serves, with the other social sciences (law, political science, and history, including importantly intellectual history) to give us insights into the human and social aspects of our environment; much more so than, say, biology. This, however, is not an invitation to push economic analysis, any more than biological, up to and beyond the limits of its applicability. Nor is it intended to suggest that *ad hoc* arbitrary mixtures of social sciences are likely to advance our understanding. It is instead a prescription to do genuine synthesis: to study these several disciplines (and others) and their implications for each other and for our total understanding of the human condition.

My other, related, themes are more narrowly focused on the question of policy. First, there is the consideration that an understanding of the legal and political background of policy — of the new political economy or public choice, if you will, ought not to emasculate us as critics of economic policy: An understanding of why governments might fail to do the economically appropriate does not require us to accept it as correct or inevitable. The technical point here is that social choice, like all normal economic analysis, takes the voter-consumers' preferences and the legal framework as given. It is one of the functions of political leadership, as it is one of ours, to educate these preferences, and, if need be, to change that framework.

Finally, there is the important injunction not to exaggerate the cataclysmic nature — the uniqueness, gravity, or permanence of our current concerns. In the transient world that we, as social scientists, deal with there are no surmountable problems and permanent solutions to them. There are only possibilities of dealing more or less satisfactorily with some minor aspects of the human condition that are, for the moment, particularly irksome.

That, to repeat, is what I think I have learnt from Scott. Others will have their own, no doubt different, lists.

Chapter V

Canada

E52
E58
E12
E13

KEYNESIAN POLICY ANALYSIS, RATIONAL EXPECTATIONS, AND THE BANK OF CANADA

Peter Howitt, University of Western Ontario

INTRODUCTION

In *The Economists Versus the Bank of Canada*, Scott Gordon explained to the general reader why in 1960 between one quarter and one third of the Canadian community of academic economists signed a letter to the Minister of Finance, in effect demanding the resignation of James Coyne, the Governor of the Bank of Canada, on grounds of incompetence. Among other charges, the economists accused Coyne of failing to understand "the mechanism by which a nation's balance of international payments is adjusted" (p. 37), maintaining the outlandish position "that inflation is a major *cause* of unemployment" (p. 14), holding the erroneous view "that combating inflation must be the paramount objective of economic policy" (p. 39), and not understanding that in conducting economic policy, "One must keep the economic situation constantly under review and be prepared to shift the gears from forward to reverse and back again as the requirements of the economy alter" (p. 13). It was obvious that someone guilty of these mistakes was unfit to be governor of a central bank.

The Keynesian analysis that lay behind the criticism of Coyne is no longer subscribed to by the vast majority of macroeconomists in Canada or the United States. It is unlikely that between one quarter and one third of Canadian academic economists would sign such a letter today. On the contrary, much of what Coyne was criticized for is now respectable macroeconomics. The idea that inflation causes unemployment has been given academic respectability by Milton Friedman's Nobel Lecture (1977), and has since won many adherents among professional economists. The idea that stabilization policy should not be adjusted continually as new information comes to light, so obviously wrong in 1960, has been promoted, first by Friedman, and then by new classical economists, as a key to sound policy making. That a central bank should ignore unemployment, so seemingly irresponsible in 1960, has become a central theorem of new classical economics (Kydland and Prescott, 1977). I suspect that a majority of Canadian macroeconomists today might even regard Coyne as having done an admirable job, for having resisted inflation against powerful opposition, of which the academic opposition was only a minor part.

In this paper I do not propose to re-examine the case against Coyne, except perhaps indirectly. Instead, my aim is to re-examine the rational-expectations critique of the Keynesian policy analysis implicit in that case, and to apply that re-examination to recent Canadian monetary policy. My main point is that rational-expectations criticisms of Keynesian policy advice can be shown to be invalid.

Specifically, even if one admits both rational expectations and the controversial Lucas aggregate supply curve at the heart of new classical economics, (a) the assumption of mechanical (structural) expectations-generating mechanisms like adaptive expectations that exist independently of the choice of policy regimes is justified, despite the famous Lucas critique; (b) the Keynesian tendency to evaluate specific policy actions rather than policy rules is justified; and (c) contrary to Kydland and Prescott a central bank will do better by continually reassessing its policy in the light of developments rather than obeying a fixed rule. I make these points by examining a conventional model of inflation and unemployment.

During the period from mid-1982 to early 1984, the Bank of Canada tried to establish its credibility by following an inflexible policy of defending the Canadian dollar against speculative pressure. Measured by almost any indicator, this rule-like policy implied an increasingly restrictive policy at a time when inflation was coming down rapidly and unemployment was near historic highs. (The parallels with the Coyne episode are obvious, but I leave them unexplored.) I shall argue that the problems which this policy encountered illustrate the fallacy of believing that considerations of expectations and credibility supplant the need for sensible Keynesian policies.

KEYNESIAN POLICY ANALYSIS

The model below is minimally sufficient to highlight those tendencies of Keynesian policy analysis that new classical economics has called into question. The following notation applies at each date t:

p_t rate of price-inflation

e_t target rate of price-inflation

p_t^e target rate of price-inflation

x_t control error, an exogenous iid random variable with mean zero

u_t rate of unemployment

b discount factor, $0 < b < 1$

v natural rate of unemployment, $v > 0$

a relative importance of inflation, $a > 0$

c speed of adaptation of expectations, $0 < c < 1$

The central bank aims at the target rate of inflation by appropriately setting its instrument (exchange rate, monetary base, or interest rate), but control error generally intervenes. Thus:

(1) $p_t = e_t + x_t$.

Since the distinction between e_t and the bank's instrument is not important for discussion, I shall treat e_t as the bank's instrument.

The trade-off between inflation and unemployment is given by an expectations-augmented Phillips curve:

(2) $u_t = v - (p_t - p_t^e)$.

Private expectations are formed adaptively:

(3) $p_{t+1}^e = p_t^e + c\,(p_t - p_t^e) = c \sum_{j=0}^{\infty} (1 - c)^j p_{t-j}$.

The bank's loss function is:

(4) $L_t = E_t \{ \sum_{i=0}^{\infty} b^i\,[(u_{t+i})^2 + a(p_{t+i})^2] \}$.

where E_t denotes the expectation conditional on the information at date t:

(5) $I_t = (p_{t-1}, p_{t-2}, ...)$.

The bank knows the parameters a,b,c,v, and the distribution of (x_t). Its decision problem at date t is to choose e_t as a function of I_t, together with a sequence of plans for each e_{t+i} as a function of I_{t+i}, so as to minimize (4) subject to (1)~(3). The unique solution to this problem is the optimal policy function:

6) $e_t = e^* + f p_t^e$,

where e^* and f are positive constants that depend on the parameters a,b,c,v.

In the special case of an infinite rate of time preference (b=0), the parameters in (6) are:

7) $e^* = v/(1+a)$, $f = 1/(1+a)$.

This myopic solution minimizes the expected loss. Note that the myopic solution applies even with a finite rate of time preference in the limiting case of a fixed expectation: $p_t^e =$ constant, or equivalently: $c=0$; in which case the bank acts myopically because its current choice of target inflation has no consequences for the trade-off it will face in the future.

There are many objectionable features of this caricature of Keynesian policy making. I would particularly question the assumptions that the bank has precise enough knowledge about the economic system and about its own objective function to formulate policy in terms of an optimal control problem, that there exists a unique natural rate of unemployment, that the bank would ideally like to reduce unemployment permanently below its natural rate,[1] and that the only source of inertia in inflation is the adjustment of expectations. Nevertheless, the model captures three important features of Keynesian policy making, to which the new classical critique has been directed.

First the bank can assume that the future evolution of the economy depends upon current policy actions, but not upon the overall strategy adopted. All intertemporal links come through the expectation equation (3). According to this equation p_{t+1}^e depends upon p_t, which in turn depends upon the current instrument-setting e_t. But the bank takes the functional form and the parameter c of this equation as given independently of its strategic choices. In modern terminology, it takes the equation as structural.

Second, policy actions can be evaluated in terms of their probable effects upon the variables of interest (in this case inflation and unemployment) without reference to any policy rule. The question of what to do now is a meaningful one, which the economist can answer by solving the dynamic programming problem for the optimal first step. A solution to this problem does not have to conform with any extraneous rule in order to be valid.

Of course the dynamic programming problem also generates a policy rule for the future; a set of plans for what to do under each contingency. That rule is fully specified by (6). But the bank is free to choose the rule. Furthermore, even if it were constrained to follow the rule in the future, it would still be free today to contemplate alternative choices of e_t. The fact that it chooses the value given by (6) today derives from a comparison of what stochastic time path inflation and unemployment would follow if it were to make that choice, compared with the path if it made any other choice today, given that in any event (6) will be obeyed in the future, not from the fact that the choice conforms with any given rule.

Third, policy actions not only can but should be evaluated in the light of the historically given situation. Bellman's principle of optimality, which governs any dynamic programming problem, states that the action chosen at any date should yield a lower loss than any other action, given that an optimal rule will be followed in the future, and taking as given the values of all variables, like p_t^e, which the decision maker is no longer free to influence; i.e. all state variables. Even though (3) states that p_t^e would have been different if actions before t had been different, it is optimal to treat bygones as bygones; to face the situation as it is, not as it might have been. The bank should continually reassess policy, and not be constrained by any extraneous rule.

CRITIQUE

The rational-expectations critique focuses on these three points.[2] It begins with the claim that expectations will be given not by the mechanical formula (3) but by rational expectations:

8) $p_t^e = E_t \cdot p_t$.

If the bank pursues the policy (6), then (1) and (8) imply:

9) $p_t^e = e^* / (1 - f)$

This unchanging expectation could be incorporated into the Keynesian analysis by assuming that $c=0$. But it implies that the expectational equation that the Keynesian analysis took as structural is not. Instead, (9) depends upon the policy parameters e^* and f. Thus treating the expectation equation as given will lead to a miscalculation of the probable consequences of alternative policy decisions. This is the essence of the Lucas critique (1976). It denies the appropriateness of the first of the above features of Keynesian policy analysis.

The second part of the rational-expectations critique was spelled out by Lucas (1980), who argued that it is pointless to discuss the consequences of, or to recommend the implementation of specific policy actions, as opposed to recommending stable, predictable rules. There are many grounds on which one might wish to impose rules on a central bank. One might believe, for example, that without specific rules the bank will act in its own self-interest rather than in the public interest, that it might become overly enthusiastic and end up doing more harm than good, or that allowing the bank much discretion is inconsistent with basic principles of constitutional democracy. To these grounds, Lucas added the following rational-expectations argument. Without fixed rules governing policy, people cannot have rational expectations, and if they do not have rational expectations we have nothing scientific to say about how they will respond to alternative policy actions in the short run. As he puts it:

> ...our ability as economists to predict the responses of agents rests, in situations where expectations about the future matter, on our understanding of the stochastic environment agents believe themselves to be operating in. In practice, this limits the class of policies the consequences of which we can hope to assess in advance to policies generated by fixed, well understood, relatively permanent rules...(p. 205)

The practical import of Lucas's thesis is to deny the appropriateness of the second of the above-mentioned features of Keynesian policy analysis. Alternative rules can be judged on the grounds of their probable consequences, using the techniques of rational expectations analysis. But specific actions can be judged, if at all, only in terms of whether or not they conform with a good rule that people have come to count on. If there is no such rule in place, then the economist has nothing to say. If there is such a rule, and it is judged to be a good one, then the only appropriate action for the policy maker to take is the one prescribed by the rule. The only remaining situation is one in which people are counting on a bad rule, in which case it follows again that the economist has nothing to say, because (1) there is no point in obeying a bad rule, but (b) we cannot predict the consequences of not obeying it.

The third part of the rational-expectations critique is attributable to Kydland and Prescott (1977). Specifically, reoptimizing every period in the light of all new information leads to suboptimal results, because of the time-consistency problem. The bank would do better to choose an optimal rule and stick to it forever no matter what new information arrives.

The argument goes as follows. The natural-rate hypothesis (2) and rational expectations (8) imply that unemployment will fluctuate randomly and uncontrollably (by the bank) around its natural rate:

10) $u_t = v - x_t$.

no matter what policy the bank follows. Thus the bank might as well minimize the cost of inflation each period and pay no attention to unemployment; the optimal rule is: $e_t = 0$.

However, a bank that followed the Keynesian analysis of the previous section would never arrive at the optimal rule. For if it did, then p_t^e would always equal zero; but then (6) would dictate $e_t = e^* > 0$. The bank would yield to the temptation to reduce unemployment temporarily by deceiving the people who were expecting zero inflation. Knowing this in advance, people would never set p_t^e equal to zero.

Instead, a Keynesian bank in a rational-expectations equilibrium will generate the target rate:

11) $e_t = v / a$

each period. In this "discretionary" equilibrium the constant expectation:

12) $p_t^e = v / a$

will be rational given (11), and the policy (11) will solve the bank's decision problem given (12).[3] In effect, the expected rate of inflation (12) is sufficiently high that the bank is no longer tempted to aim for an even higher target.

If the bank could somehow commit itself to setting $e_t = 0$ — to resisting the temptation to inflate — it would be better off. Unemployment would be the same each period, and inflation would be less, by the amount

v/a. The extra loss from being free to reoptimize is:

$$L_t^{\text{discretion}} - L_t^{\text{commitment}} = E_t \sum_{i=0}^{\infty} b^i a \{[(v/a) + x_{t+i}]^2 - x_{t+i}^2\} = v^2 /a(1-b) > 0.$$

Thus Kydland and Prescott deny the appropriateness of the third feature of Keynesian analysis.

THE RATIONAL-EXPECTATIONS DEFENCE OF KEYNESIAN POLICY ANALYSIS

For the sake of argument I accept all the assumptions of the above critique. To these assumptions I add one more, that the central bank has no legal constraints preventing it from reoptimizing every period. It cannot build a doomsday machine that will automatically inflict infinite punishment on it if it operates rationally in the light of a historically given situation. This assumption is well grounded in the facts. The legal constraints imposed upon the Bank of Canada by the preamble to the Bank of Canada Act[4] are too vague to constitute any limitation on its discretion. While it is true that during the 1981-82 recession the Bank resisted an enormous political pressure to reflate, it is also true that any time it has attempted to stake its reputation to a narrowly prescribed policy, it has ended up abandoning that policy, as in the case of Monetary Gradualism with its targets for M-1 growth rates, and again with its policy of fiercely resisting currency depreciation in the 1980-84 period.

Given these assumptions, the defence of Keynesian analysis is straightforward. Accept the Kydland-Prescott argument that the discretionary equilibrium described by (11) and (12) will be attained. It is crucial to that argument that the bank take equation (12) as given; that it takes as given that expected inflation will equal the exogenous constant v/a, this period, next period, and forever. For only under this assumption does (11) minimize the bank's loss, as required by the conditions of equilibrium.

The Kydland-Prescott assumption that the bank takes (12) as given makes perfectly good sense in the context. It means just that (a) people do not have the flexibility to change p_t^e after e_t has been set, and (b) they can calculate that the bank will always choose (11), which together with (1) implies that (12) is the only rational expectation. Nothing the bank says or does can alter (a) or (b), so nothing it says or does can alter (12).

It follows that the Lucas critique is invalid. For the Kydland-Prescott assumption is equivalent to saying that the bank should treat (12) as structural. Just as in the caricature of Keynesian policy making, the bank should take as given the form of the equation determining the evolution of expectations, as well as the numerical values of the parameters in the equation, independently of its own policy choices.

It also follows that the second part of the rational-expectations critique is wrong. In the discretionary equilibrium people can and do form rational expectations. Thus, contrary to Lucas's claim, the consequences of isolated actions by the bank can be assessed, using the tools of rational-expectations analysis, even though the bank is not committed to any rule. Specifically, it follows from (1), (2), and (12) that whatever value of e_t the bank chooses, the rate of inflation will equal $e_t + x_t$ and the rate of unemployment will equal $(1+a)\ v/a - e_t - x_t$.

Finally, it also follows that the third part of the critique is wrong. The fact that the bank can take (12) as given means it can do nothing better than minimize its loss, in the light of the historically given situation (in particular, taking the current p_t^e as given), unconstrained by any other rule, exactly as it does in the discretionary equilibrium. The outcome will be a rate of inflation equal to $v/a + x_t$, by (1) and (11), and a rate of unemployment equal to $v - x_t$, by (10). If the bank tried to improve upon this by adopting the Kydland-Prescott rule, then according to the results of the preceding paragraph, inflation would fall to x_t but unemployment would rise to $(1+a)v/a - x_t$. Each period the expected loss would increase by the amount:

$$E_t\{[(1+a)v/a - x_t]^2 + ax_t^2 - [v-x_t]^2 - a[v/a + x_t]^2\} = (1+a)(v/a)^2 > 0.$$

Thus the Kydland-Prescott critique is invalid on its own terms.

REPUTATION — BUILDING A DOOMSDAY MACHINE

What would happen if the bank were to ignore everything I have said, and stubbornly refuse to reoptimize each period, even without the aid of a doomsday machine, in the hope that my analysis is wrong, and that it can build a reputation as an inflation fighter that will, at least eventually, affect expectations and improve the trade-off? Would people not eventually give in to the weight of evidence and reduce their expectations? And if so would that not make such a policy rational, in contradiction to what I have argued?

There are at least two ways of addressing this question. Both, I shall argue, end up with the same conclusion as the above defence, although they do require some qualification. The first is to examine whether the bank could in effect build a doomsday machine out of whole cloth, by making the following announcement. Count on us to deliver the Kydland-

Prescott rule. As long as you observe us following the rule, count on us to continue following the rule. But if ever you see that we have violated the rule, then we deserve to lose our reputation; don't ever believe us again. Instead, assume that we will go back forever to the inferior discretionary equilibrium.

If people are willing to start out on this course, then the bank will have constructed a doomsday machine. If ever the bank yields to the temptation to behave opportunistically, to aim for a rate of unemployment below the natural rate, it will risk being found out, and losing its reputation forever. Losing its reputation would mean that the superior outcome of the rational-expectations equilibrium under the Kydland-Prescott, by following a rule and giving up discretion.

For such a plan to work, people would have to be persuaded somehow to adopt the expectational scheme the bank has proposed. This raises two distinct questions, one easier to answer than the other. The first, easier question is whether such a scheme would constitute a rational expectation. The answer is yes, provided again that the discount factor is close enough to unity. The question has been addressed by several papers in the credibility literature, so I will just illustrate with a simple example.

Specifically, suppose that there is no control error. This eliminates the public's difficulty in inferring from the observed history of p_t whether the bank has been following the Kydland-Prescott rule. Any deviation will be detected immediately. Then as long as the bank has maintained its reputation it can keep inflation equal to zero and unemployment equal to its natural rate v forever by honouring its commitment to setting $e_t = 0$ each period. This would yield a loss equal to $v^2/(1-b)$. But once it has lost its reputation the best it can do is stick to the discretionary equilibrium, with a rate of inflation equal to v/a and the same unemployment rate v, hence a loss of $(1+a)v^2/(1-b)$.

Thus the cost of losing its reputation will be that from next period forward the loss will be greater by the amount of $av^2/(1-b)$. Discounted back to this period the cost is av^2/r, where $b = 1/(1+r)$. On the other hand, there is a gain to losing its reputation because it can exploit a favourable trade-off once. With p_t^e fixed at zero, the bank would set e_t equal to $v/(1+a)$, the value given the myopic rule of (6) and (7), thereby reducing unemployment to $v-v/(1+a)$ and raising inflation to $v/(1+a)$. The short-run gain would be:

$$v^2 - [v - v/(1+a)]^2 - a[v/(1+a)]^2 = v^2/(1+a) > 0.$$

Accordingly the bank will find it optimal to keep its reputation if $v^2/(1+a)$ $< av^2/r$, that is, if $r<a(1+a)$.

The second and much harder question is why people would adopt this scheme in preference to any other rational scheme. For as we have seen, the fixed expectation (12) is also a rational scheme. That is, there is more than one rational-expectations equilibrium. Is there anything that would make the doomsday equilibrium somehow more likely to be selected than any other?

What makes this a difficult question to answer on theoretical grounds is that economics has little to say about which equilibrium will be selected when many exist. Perhaps a central bank could use its prominence to act as a Schelling-like focal point for expectations to help pick a good one, by announcing that it will be behaving in a way compatible with its preferred one. But there is no reason to believe that it always can. People are not compelled to form their expectations the way the bank wants them to, even if to do so would be compatible with the conditions of rational-expectations equilibrium. They might choose to ignore what the bank says, as in the discretionary equilibrium. We just do not know under precisely what conditions central bank announcements will be regarded by the public as credible.

The doomsday equilibrium would look more plausible if people could be led to form these expectations not through exhortation but through experience, using some plausible learning mechanism.[5] But that seems unlikely, because of the discontinuous nature of the expectations. Once any deviation at all from the Kydland-Prescott rule is observed beliefs must make a quantum change and never return to what they were. It is hard to imagine what experience could conceivably lead people to form such discontinuous beliefs except the observation that slight deviations from the ideal rule have in fact been followed by very long periods of high inflation. But if people had made such observations, what would lead them now to believe that the long periods were about to come to an end, as they must in the doomsday equilibrium? Apocalyptic beliefs are not unknown, but they are acquired by faith, not by experience.[6]

On the other hand, there is a simple learning mechanism that would lead to the discretionary equilibrium. Suppose people believe that their observations of price-inflation are being drawn from an unchanging distribution. The belief will be wrong in the short run but not, as we shall see, in the long run. Given this belief, a natural way of predicting inflation is to take an unweighted average of past values. Likewise, suppose that the central bank believes that p_t^e is a serially uncorrelated random variable, independent of the bank's actions. This belief too will be wrong in the short run but not in the long run.

Under these assumptions each period expectations will adjust according to the formula:

(13) $p_t^e = p_{t-1}^e + (1/t)[p_{t-1} - p_{t-1}^e]$.

Each period the bank will find it optimal to follow the myopic rule, given by (6) and (7); thus:

(14) $p_t = (p_t^e + v)/(1+a)$.

From (13) and (14):

(15) $p_t^e - p_{t-1}^e = (1/t)[(p_{t-1}^e + v)/(1+a) - p_{t-1}^e]$.

It is easily shown that the sequence of expectations governed by (15) converges asymptotically to the expectation in the discretionary equilibrium: $p_t^e = v/a$.

The reputation model of this section thus provides little support for the message of Kydland and Prescott. Perhaps a central bank could persuade people to adopt doomsday expectations, and then the discretionary equilibrium could be improved upon. But this would require people to place a great deal of weight on central bank announcements, and there is no compelling reason in general to think that they will. If people must learn by experience rather than by listening to the bank, then it seems highly unlikely that they would ever stumble upon doomsday expectations. Instead it seems more likely that they would stumble upon the expectations of the discretionary equilibrium.

Furthermore, it should be noted that even if somehow the doomsday equilibrium were attained, the three rational-expectations criticisms of Keynesian policy analysis would still not be correct. For in the doomsday equilibrium the expectational rule, which is known to the bank, determines a relationship between today's instrument setting and the future evolution of expectations which the bank can legitimately treat as structural; namely that expected inflation will equal zero until the instrument deviates from zero, and will equal v/a from then on. Also, the consequences of taking alternative actions today can be calculated, as we did when evaluating the condition for the equilibrium to be incentive compatible. Finally, the bank should continually reoptimize each period, as indeed it does in the doomsday equilibrium, taking the expectational rule as given. Provided that $r < a(1+a)$ this optimization will arrive at the result each period that it is optimal to stick to the Kydland-Prescott rule.

REPUTATION — EDUCATING THE PUBLIC

Another way to address the reputation question is to suppose that the public is uncertain about the exact nature of the loss function being minimized by the central bank. Specifically,[7] suppose that the first term in the loss function is not the square of the unemployment rate but instead the squared deviation from some ideal rate z. Then z will be an inverse measure of the bank's incentive to exploit a favourable trade-off. In the preceding analysis z was equal to zero and the incentive existed. But if z were equal to the natural rate of unemployment v there would be no incentive; when p_t^e equalled zero the bank would prefer to aim at zero inflation.

Suppose that the exact value of z is known only to the central bank. The public must try to infer z from observing the rate of inflation, which provides only a noisy signal. If people could see the instrument setting e_t they could infer z, but they see only the sum $e_t + x_t$. Suppose that z follows a random walk:

$$z_t = z_{t-1} + w_t$$

where w_t is exogenous white noise. Then it can be shown that there is an equilibrium of the form:

$$(16) \quad e_t = e^* + \alpha z_t + f p_t^e, \quad \alpha > 0,$$

in which people form expectations adaptively, according to (3).

In this equilibrium, the policy (16) minimizes the bank's expected loss subject to (1) ~ (3). In the special case where $z_t = 0$ it reduces to (6). Also (3) constitutes a rational expectation in this case, for the same reason as in Muth (1960). The variable people are trying to forecast is

$$y_t \equiv \alpha z_t + x_t$$

because:

$$p_t = e_t + x_t = e^* + f p_t^e + y_t.$$

The past history of y_t is the only useful information in making this forecast. Since y_t is a random walk plus white noise, the rational expectation has the form (3), where the parameter c depends upon the ratio of the variance of the control error to the variance of the innovations in αz_t.

When $z_t = v$, the bank really is trying to bring inflation down to zero ($e^* + \alpha z = 0$). There would be no time-consistency problem if only people knew the truth. But they do not. Instead, the bank has a reputation, in the form of the estimated value $E_t z_t$ underlying expected inflation. No central bank announcement that $z = v$ will be believed because it would clearly be in the interests of the bank to make the announcement even if it were not true. People will change their minds only by having their expectations disconfirmed by experience.

Again it is not optimal to adopt the Kydland-Prescott rule. Instead, if people are expecting positive inflation then it is optimal for the bank to educate them gradually. That is, since $f > 0$, an optimal planned path of disinflation does not aim to accomplish its goal in one period. Disinflation raises unemployment above the natural rate, with therefore a positive marginal cost, whereas once inflation has been brought down to zero there is no marginal gain from further reductions. This more plausible-looking model of reputation gives even less support, then, for the Kydland-Prescott argument for rules over discretion. As with the previous model, the analysis also refutes the three rational-expectations criticisms of Keynesian analysis. The bank can take the expectation equation (3) as structural, since it will not be affected in this equilibrium by the bank's overall strategy, only by the value αz that people have calculated. It can therefore use this equation to assess the consequences of different actions today even though it is not committed to any monetary rule. And it should reoptimize every period, since not to do so would unambiguously raise the loss.

THE ECONOMIC CONSEQUENCES OF NEW CLASSICAL ECONOMICS

The preceding analysis has argued that the new classical critique is invalid under its own assumptions if the central bank has no power of commitment, even taking reputational considerations into account. In particular, it will not be optimal for the bank to follow the Kydland-Prescott rule. But I still have not fully answered the question of what would happen if the bank persisted in ignoring Keynesian advice and followed the rule anyway. Given that to do so would be incompatible with rational behaviour, what would be the consequences of this irrationality?

On the one hand, if the bank could be counted on to behave irrationally forever, then the force of repeated experience with zero inflation would eventually persuade people to expect zero inflation unconditionally, even though that is incompatible with the conditions of rational-expectations equilibrium. The inevitable conclusion would be that irrational behaviour is preferable to rational behaviour, at least in the long run.[8]

This is not entirely out of the question. We all know individuals who have remained faithful to irrational principles throughout their lives. But most central banks, certainly including the Bank of Canada, are not like that. The political and social pressures on them to respond to inflation and unemployment in the light of given circumstances, together with the social commitment and intelligence of their officials, make sheer obstinacy an unlikely assumption. Coyne came perhaps as close to that ideal as possible. The fact that he was replaced before long helps to make his the exception that proves the rule.

Thus it seems that the consequence of being persuaded by rational-expectations arguments that a Kydland-Prescott rule should be followed even when it is not time-consistent is that sooner or later the combination of political and social pressure and good sense will cause the policy to be abandoned in favour of something closer to an optimal reaction function. In this section of the paper I explore what will happen if the public has rational expectations about the likelihood that the bank's irrational commitment to a rule will give way to good Keynesian advice.

Specifically, I continue to maintain the assumptions on which the new classical critique is based, but in addition assume that the bank is sticking to the rule: $e_t = 0$ until the rule is abandoned in favour of a rational Keynesian policy. Suppose that the probability of rationality being restored next period is equal to the constant $1 - \emptyset$ as long as the rule lasts. (This probability could be made to depend upon the rate of unemployment with little effect on the results.) Suppose also that when restoration occurs people will realize with certainty that it has occurred, but with a one-period lag.

Once restoration has taken place and everyone realizes it, the economy will revert to the discretionary equilibrium, with $e_t = v/a = p_t$ and $p_t = v/a + x_t$. But during the period of restoration the bank will follow the policy: $e_t = (v + p_t^e)/(1 + a)$ that minimizes its current loss with no consequences for the future.

At each date until the period after restoration, people's expectations will be formed as follows. Let q_t be the probability that the rule is still being followed at date t, conditional on private information I_t. Then:

(17) $p_t^e = (1-q_t)(p_t^e + v)/(1 + a) = v(1 - q_t)/(a + q_t) > 0$.

Thus the expected rate of inflation will be a decreasing function of the probability q_t. The rate of inflation will equal the control error x_t, and the rate of unemployment will equal:

$$u_t = v + p_t^e - p_t = v + p_t^e - x_t = v\,(a+1)/(a+q_t) - x_t$$

which will be greater than the natural rate on average, and also a decreasing function of the probability q_t.

Bayes' Rule can be used (see Appendix) to derive the following formula for q_t:

(18) $$q_t = \frac{g(x_{t-1})\emptyset^2}{g(x_{t-1})\emptyset + g\,[x_{t-1} - (p_{t-1}^e + v)/(1 + a)](1 - \emptyset)}$$

where g is the density of the control error. Equation (18) can be substituted into (17) to express this period's expectation as a function of last period's expectation and last period's control error. The random component of inflation will affect this period's expectation because people cannot tell for sure whether it was a control error under the rule or whether instead it might signal that the rule has been dropped.

Thus inflation will fluctuate around zero, but unemployment will fluctuate around a level higher than the natural rate. Expectations of inflation will stubbornly fluctuate around a positive mean despite the actual experience of zero inflation on average.

RECENT CANADIAN EXPERIENCE

The preceding analysis sheds some light on the Canadian experience from mid-1982 to early 1984. During the period the Bank of Canada clung stubbornly to an inflexible policy of defending the value of the Canadian dollar. Inflation came down sharply from its levels of 1981. Unemployment remained abnormally high. But the Bank stuck to its policy, despite the fact that by most measures that fixed policy implied an increasingly restrictive stance at a time when restriction was becoming less defensible from a Keynesian perspective. I have described the details of this experience elsewhere. (Howitt, 1986).

The Bank's defence of its policies invoked the reputational considerations involved in the new classical critique. In mid-1984 the Governor of the Bank, Gerald Bouey stated that:

A prescription for [expansionary monetary policy] would bring the Canadian dollar under intense downward pressure once it became evident that there was no policy concern about the Canadian dollar and the impact of any decline on inflation. In a situation where Canadian policy was perceived to be oriented towards repeating the inflationary mistakes of the 1970s, the exchange rate decline would have no evident limit. Interest rates would in fact rise sharply rather than fall as investors sought to get out of assets denominated in a currency that was only headed in a downward direction and as financial markets came to be dominated by the unpleasant prospect of much higher inflation rates. (Bouey, 1984, p. 9)

Meanwhile, unemployment fluctuated around a level that all agreed was unnaturally high, and, as the Bank frequently observed, expectations of much higher inflation stubbornly persisted. These expectations were reflected in strong speculative pressure in the foreign exchange market. The Bank had to intervene frequently and massively to forestall speculative runs on the dollar.

The Bank invoked those speculative pressures as a justification of its hard-line policy. It argued that abandonment of its policy in favour of Keynesian policies would lead to expected depreciation, and ultimately to inflation, "with no evident limit." It pointed in particular to what had happened on various occasions when people had seen the dollar decline a little and had obviously extrapolated these declines into the future. It argued that because of this extreme sensitivity of expectations to perception of policy, an inflexible policy was needed to keep expectations from worsening the policy dilemma permanently. Indeed the Bank went beyond rational expectations to argue that an inflexible policy was needed to prevent what was in effect extrapolative expectations from leading to explosive instability.[9]

The analysis of the preceding section provides a distorted picture of the episode in many respects.[10] However it offers an alternative interpretation of this extreme sensitivity of expectations to any hint of inflation. It suggests that sensitivity was not an indication that an inflexible policy was best, or that instability of expectations necessitated Bank intervention, but a sign that people did not believe that the Bank would persist forever in being irrational. For under a weak additional assumption[11] on the density g, equations (17) and (18) predict that random increase in inflation in period $t - 1$ will cause people to raise their expectation of inflation in period *t*, even though that expectation was already higher than average experience. People would take the increase in inflation as a signal that perhaps reason was being restored to policy making.

The reasonableness of this alternative interpretation is strengthened by the fact that the Bank's rigid policy ultimately was in fact abandoned. Starting in the first quarter of 1984 the value of the Canadian dollar, as measured by the Bank's own G-10 weighted average rate, began to fall from the narrow band around which it had been kept since late 1978, until by the end of 1987 it stood about twelve percentage points lower. Those who had bet on rational Keynesian policies being restored did not lose money.

CONCLUSION

Rational expectations, far from undermining Keynesian policy analysis, in fact support it. A mistaken belief in the rational expectations critique led the Bank of Canada into policies that are subject to Keynesian criticism in the 1980s. But this does not imply that we should revert to the Keynesianism of the early 1960s, or that we have learned nothing since. Indeed we have learned a lot, much of it from rational-expectations theorists, and much of it suggesting that the activism of early Keynesianism was misplaced.

One thing we learned from the experience of stagflation in the 1970s is that probably very little of what we believe about the nature of the economic system is right. Given the inability of the entire profession to predict that experience in advance, huge standard errors should be attached to the coefficients in any model used for Keynesian policy analysis. Another thing that we have learned, or more accurately relearned, is that ultimately, excessive monetary expansion is guaranteed to cause high inflation. The combination of these two lessons argues strongly for a monetary policy aimed primarily at controlling the rate of monetary expansion, and reacting only in exceptional circumstances to the pressures of unemployment. This is a far cry from the advice to "shift the gears from forward to reverse and back again as the requirements of the economy alter."[12]

Nor does this defence of the Keynesian focus on specific policy actions rather than on fixed rules imply that economists should stop advocating broad institutional reform. The rational-expectations literature has taught us much about what sorts of reform might be useful for monetary policy. For example, as Rogoff (1985) and others have pointed out, appointing as head of the central bank an obviously insensitive person that gives little thought to the plight of the unemployed, and giving that person large measure of independence from the political process is one way of approaching the Kydland-Prescott ideal, although, as Rogoff also points out, there is a cost to this suggestion, namely that such a person would not respond optimally to information which is private to the central bank. Likewise, in cases where fiscal deficits are exerting pressure on the central bank, fiscal reforms can undoubtedly improve the rational-expectations equilibrium by reducing expected inflation.

Finally, the important idea that a central bank, or more generally a government, could act as a focal point to help the economy select a good rational-expectations equilibrium in the case of multiple equilibria is an extremely important message. Whether it will or will not work in any specific case is hard to judge. It did not seem to work for the Bank of Canada during Monetary Gradualism or during the 1982-84 period. But we understand too little about what makes some announcements credible and others not, to dismiss the idea entirely.

Thus the message of the present paper is just that it does more harm than good for a policy maker to pretend that it has credibility when it obviously does not. Facts should be faced as they are, in the light of actual circumstances, not as they might have been under some ideal rule. My main criticism of the rational-expectations critique is that it has obscured this simple but important message.

APPENDIX

Equation (18) can be derived as follows. By assumption, people know that the rule was still being followed at t-2. Thus before p_{t-1} was observed, the probability that the rule was being followed at t-1 was the constant Ø. So, by Bayes' Rule, the probability that the rule was being followed at t-1, after p_{t-1} is observed is:

Prob {Rule being followed at t-1 | p_{t-1}}

$$= \frac{f[p_{t-1}|e_{t-1} = 0]Ø}{f[p_{t-1}| e_{t-1} = 0]Ø + f[p_{t-1}|e_{t-1} = (p_{t-1}^{e} + v)/(1+a)](1-Ø)}$$

where $f[p_{t-1}|e_{t-1}]$ is the conditional density of p_{t-1}. Since $p_{t-1} = e_{t-1} + x_{t-1}$, therefore the conditional density f is equal to $g(p_{t-1} - e_{t-1})$, where g is the (unconditional) density of x_{t-1}. Thus:

Prob {Rule being followed at t-1 | p_{t-1}} =

$$= \frac{g(p_{t-1})Ø}{g(p_{t-1})Ø + g[p_{t-1} - (p_{t-1}^{e} + v)/(1+a)](1-Ø)}$$

Recall that $p_{t-1} = x_{t-1}$ until restoration occurs, and that:

q_t = Prob {Rule being followed at t-1 | p_{t-1}} x Ø.

Equation (18) follows directly.

NOTES

[1]   That is, $\partial L_t / \partial u_t > 0 \; u_t \, \varepsilon \, (0, v]$.

[2]   Also on the related policy-ineffectiveness proposition, which is not addressed in this paper. However, both Lucas and Sargent have denied that policy-effectiveness is central to their work. See Klamer (1984).

[3]   The solution is given by (6) and (7), because p_t^e is constant. Substituting (12) into (7) yields (11).

[4]   The preamble indicates that the Bank is "to regulate credit and currency in the best interests of the economic life of the nation, to control and protect the external value of the national monetary unit and to mitigate by its influence fluctuations in the general level of production, trade, prices and employment, so far as may be possible within the scope of monetary action, and generally to promote the economic and financial welfare of the Dominion."

[5]   This criterion for choosing among multiple rational-expectations equilibria has also been advocated by Lucas (1986) and Marcet and Sargent (1986).

[6]   There is also the matter of the "sunspot" nature of the doomsday equilibrium. That is, people must condition their expectations on something other than the fundamental state variables of the economy. Following the first deviation from the Kydland-Prescott rule, the same central bank would be in the same situation, with the same objective function, as the previous period, if only people formed the same expectation as the previous period. Yet people change their expectations anyway. Thus they are conditioning their expectations on an extraneous piece of information (previous deviation from the rule) which, if they were ignoring it, would not matter for anything that anyone cares about. However, I do not find this to be grounds for rejecting the doomsday equilibrium independently of its lack of stability under learning. The results of Woodford (1987) and Howitt and McAfee (1988) show that in some cases people would be led by plausible learning mechanisms into sunspot equilibria in other contexts.

[7]   The model sketched here derives from Howitt (1987), who shows the existence of an equilibrium of the form (16) under a slightly different specification of the inflation-unemployment mechanism. The approach

is also similar to that of Cukierman and Meltzer (1986) who assume that the loss function is linear, rather than quadratic, in unemployment, and who treat a rather than z as stochastic.

[8] Rose (1989) would undoubtedly argue that therefore the behaviour was in fact rational.

[9] See, for example, Bank of Canada (1984, pp. 7-10, 17-20).

[10] See above, p. 5 in particular the expectations-augmented Phillips curve (2) has too simple a dynamic structure to capture the nature of the policy problem, which was not that the Bank was aiming at too low a target for inflation but that it was trying to reach the target too soon.

[11] Specifically, the monotone likelihood ratio property familiar from the principle-agent literature. See Grossman and Hart (1983). This property would be satisfied, for example, if the control error were normally distributed.

[12] It should be noted that the kind of monetary policy I am suggesting here is also the kind that the current Governor of the Bank, John Crow, outlined in his Eric Hanson Memorial Lecture (1988), and that the Bank seems to have been following sine then.

REFERENCES

Bank of Canada, *Annual Repot* 1984.

Bouey, Gerald, K., "Address to the Board of Directors of the Bank of Canada," *Bank of Canada Review* (July 1984), pp 3-8.

Canzoneri, Matthew B., "Monetary Policy Games and the Role of Private Information," *American Economic Review* 75 (December 1985), pp. 1056-70.

Crow, John W., "The Work of Canadian Monetary Policy," Eric J. Hanson Memorial Lecture, reprinted in *Bank of Canada Review* (February 1988), pp. 3-17.

Cukierman, Alex, "Central Bank Behavior and Credibility — Some Recent Theoretical Developments," *Federal Reserve Bank of St. Louis Review* 68 (May 1986), pp. 5-17.

_____, and Allan H. Meltzer, "A Theory of Ambiguity, Credibility and Inflation Under Discretion and Asymmetric Information," *Econometrica* 54 (September 1986), pp. 1099-1128.

Fischer, Stanley, "Time Consistent Monetary and Fiscal Policies: A Survey," mimeo, MIT, 1986.

Friedman, Milton, "Inflation and Unemployment," *Journal of Political Economy* 85 (June 1977), pp. 451-72.

Gordon, H. Scott, *The Economists versus the Bank of Canada*. Toronto: Ryerson Press, 1961.

Grossman, Sanford, J., and Oliver Hart, "An Analysis of the Principle - Agent Problem," *Econometrica* 51 (January 1983), pp. 7-45.

Howitt, Peter, *Monetary Policy in Transition: A Study of Bank of Canada Policy 1982-85*. Toronto: C.D. Howe Institute, 1986.

_____, "Optimal Disinflation in a Small Open Economy," mimeo, University of Western Ontario, 1987.

_____, and R. Preston McAfee, "Animal Spirits," mimeo, University of Western Ontario, 1988.

Klamer, Arjo, *Conversations with Economists*. Totowa, N.J.: Rowman and Allanheld, 1984.

Kydland, Finn, and Edward Prescott, "Rules rather than Discretion: The Inconsistency of Optimal Plans," *Journal of Political Economy* 85 (June 1977), pp. 473-91.

Lucas, Robert E. Jr., "Econometric Policy Evaluation: A Critique," in Karl Brunner and Allan Meltzer, eds., *The Phillips Curve and Labor Markets*. Vol. no. 1 of Carnegie-Rochester Conference Series on Public Policy, Amsterdam: North-Holland, 1976.

_____, "Rules, Discretion, and the Role of the Economic Advisor," In Stanley Fischer, ed., *Rational Expectations and Economic Policy*. Chicago: University of Chicago Press (for NBER), 1980.

_____, "Adaptive Behavior and Economic Theory," *Journal of Business* 59 (October 1986), pp. S401-S426.

McCallum, Bennett T., "Credibility and Monetary Policy," In *Price Stability and Public Policy*. Kansas City: Federal Reserve Bank of Kansas City, 1984.

Marcet, Albert, and Thomas Sargent, "Convergence of Least Squares Learning Mechanisms in Self Referential Linear Stochastic Models," mimeo, Hoover Institution, 1986.

Muth, John, "Optimal Properties of Exponentially Weighted Forecasts," *Journal of the American Statistical Association* 55 (June 1960), pp. 299-306.

Rogoff, Kenneth, "The Optimal Degree of Commitment to an Intermediate Monetary Target," *Quarterly Journal of Economics* 100 (November 1985), pp. 1169-89.

_____, "Reputational Constraints on Monetary Policy," In Karl Brunner and Allan Meltzer eds., *Bubbles and Other Essays*. Vol. no. 26 of Carnegie-Rochester Conference Series on Public Policy, Amsterdam: North-Holland, 1987.

Rowe, P. Nicholas, *Rules and Institutions*. Oxford: Philip Allan, 1989.

Woodford, Michael, "Learning to Believe in Sunspots," unpublished, University of Chicago, 1987.

p 95.

COMMENTS ON PETER HOWITT'S PAPER

David Longworth*, Bank of Canada
and
Nicholas Rowe, Carleton University

DAVID LONGWORTH

In these comments, which represent my own views and not necessarily those of the Bank of Canada, I will follow the same general outline as Peter Howitt used in his paper:

1. the case against Coyne;
2. the rational-expectations critique of Keynesian policy analysis;
3. recent Canadian monetary policy; and
4. comments on other aspects of Keynesian policy analysis.

1. THE CASE AGAINST COYNE

As one of the younger members of this gathering, I was only nine years old in 1961 and remember nothing first-hand about the Coyne affair. I imagine that I first came across references to the Coyne affair and Scott Gordon in reading Peter Newman's book *Renegade in Power* in my high school days. More recently, in re-examining the Bank of Canada's relationship with academics as background reading for the Governor's speech to the Canadian Economics Association in June, I had occasion to read for the first time Scott Gordon's book *The Economists versus the Bank of Canada.* I found it valuable because it helped to drive home the point that critical commentary can be useful in understanding ongoing developments and in helping to avoid mistakes in the future. Both Scott Gordon and Peter Howitt have been valued critics of the Bank of Canada in this sense.

---

* The views expressed in this comment are those of the author and no responsibility for them should be attributed to the Bank of Canada.

James Coyne's views on open economy macroeconomics were far from the mainstream in the late 1950s.[1] In the end, however, that was not his downfall as much as his appearance of "sheer obstinacy" to which Howitt alludes. It is of interest that the lasting legacy of the Coyne affair was a clarification of the responsibility for monetary policy that was later enshrined in law.[2]

One question, however, remains. Was Coyne, in spite of what proved to be incorrect analysis in the domain of international macroeconomics and the appearance of "sheer obstinacy," correct in placing a greater weight on the perils of inflation than his contemporaries? Howitt does not attempt to answer this question, but perhaps I could tempt him to explore this more fully at some future time.

2. THE RATIONAL-EXPECTATIONS DEFENCE OF KEYNESIAN POLICY ANALYSIS

In the main body of his paper, Howitt shows that Keynesian policy analysis can be defended in rational-expectations models if everyone agrees on the appropriate loss function and if the central bank itself has rational expectations and no legal constraints preventing it from reoptimizing every period. This is because if the bank is a rational actor, then others will be able to calculate its reaction function. One will therefore have a "perfect equilibrium." Three points then follow:

   i.   the Lucas critique is invalid;
   ii   it is possible for the analyst to take into account the consequences of isolated policy actions; and
   iii. the Kydland-Prescott critique that dynamic programming is suboptimal because it is time-inconsistent is invalid.

Howitt then extends his model in a number of ways:

   i.   He examines whether a central bank could persuade people to adopt "doomsday" expectations so that the equilibrium of discretion could be improved upon. He notes that this would require people to place *a great deal of weight* on central bank announcements and there is no compelling reason in general to think that they will. To which I would add that neither is there clear evidence from Canadian experience that they would.
   ii. He shows that if people expect positive inflation then the bank should educate them gradually, pursuing disinflation over more than one period. This is certainly accepted by the Bank of Canada in its move to price stability.

Up to this point, Howitt has used a simple model to make his points. He beats the rational-expectations advocates on their own ground, so to speak, and his argumentation is valid. But he never tells us whether he believes that individuals and central banks do have rational expectations and, if so, in what sense.[3,4] Nor does he examine more thoroughly the loss function he has assumed — including whether central bank behaviour is described by such a function and how private agents can determine the loss function that the central bank is using if there is potentially more than one parameter that has changed over time. Without some discussion of these points, it is not immediately clear why one would want to apply the simple model outlined in the paper to the real world situation of Canadian monetary policy in the 1982-84 period. In the first instance, this is a plea for justification of why it is appropriate to use his simple model to examine the world. But in the second instance, as I will try to make clear, there are good reasons to believe that real world complications may invalidate inferences made from the model.

First, one can explore what happens if one generalizes the loss function from:

$$L_t = E_t^g SUM_i \{b^i [(u_{t+1})^2 + a (p_{t+1})^2]\}.$$

to

$$L_t = E_t^g SUM_i \{b^i [(u_{t+i} - v_t + d_t)^2 + a (p_{t+i} - p'_t)^2]\},$$

where v_t is the perceived natural rate of unemployment at time t, d_t ($0 < d_t < v_t$) adjusts the natural rate to an unemployment target that may differ from the natural rate, and p'_t is the desired inflation rate. (It is assumed that the authorities always set the future values v_{t+i}, d_{t+i}, and p'_{t+i} equal to the current values v_t, d_t, and p'_t, respectively.)

Then, in general, it is possible not only that the authorities may change their perceptions of v_t through time (a case which Howitt examines), but their values of d_t, p'_t and a as well. It then becomes difficult for the public to disentangle any changes in these four parameters.[5] This, as I argue below, may have implications for central bank pronouncements.

3. RECENT CANADIAN MONETARY POLICY

Peter Howitt makes the assumption that in making pronouncements in 1982-84, the Bank was invoking reputational considerations involved in the new classical critique. An alternative view is that the Bank was attempting to indicate something about its model of the world and something about its "loss function,"[6] in particular that a (the weight on inflation) was high and p'_t (the target inflation rate) was low.[7] This might be a not unreasonable way to proceed if people do not form expectations solely in mechanical mathematical ways based only on the past history of prices, wages, and the unemployment rate and on a model whose structure (although not parameters) is known with certainty.[8] When there are a lot of parameters to be estimated in a regression equation it is sometimes helpful to have a prior distribution. Perhaps pronouncements can influence that prior distribution, while at the same time not influencing the formation of price expectations directly.

More generally, it is not surprising that central banks would like to establish credibility with respect to their desire for low inflation, even if it is not entirely clear how this can be done. Making clear what one is trying to do does not imply that one believes that credibility is easily bought or that one believes the new classical critique.

The Bank of Canada was not following an explicit rule for the exchange rate, or for money, or for inflation in the 1982-84 period. However, it is clear to me that expansionary monetary policy would have led to more inflation, particularly given the expectational situation at the time. Furthermore, because of random errors, one cannot conclude that the unemployment-inflation outcome was the one that the Bank desired.

4. Concluding Remarks on Keynesianism

If you have gathered that there are Keynesian elements in the analysis of the economy among some of the staff at the Bank of Canada — myself included — you have gathered correctly. Prices are sticky, expectations are not always rational (in a strong sense), new classical critiques of Keynesian analysis are overstated, rules are not always to be preferred to discretion — these ideas are not to be frowned upon. And yet, clearly, Bank policy does not follow the Keynesian prescriptions of the 1950s and 1960s. As Peter Howitt says, "Indeed we have learned a lot, much of it from rational-expectations theorists, and much of it suggesting that the activism of early Keynesianism was misplaced." He goes on to add that "probably very little of what we believe about the nature of the economic system is right," but admits that "excessive monetary expansion is guaranteed ultimately to cause high inflation."

As Howitt argues, these factors would suggest the avoidance of excessive gear shifting (thus eschewing fine tuning for better outcomes over the medium term), but also would not suggest the abandonment of good sense in favour of some rigid rule.[9] This, as he mentions in a footnote, is the kind of policy that Governor John Crow has outlined. In the real world where one can build forecasts of future inflation based not only on past price inflation, past wage inflation and unemployment, but on monetary aggregates, nominal spending, and capacity utilization, one wants to be looking at all those additional variables too. The Bank of Canada does not have a rule for a monetary aggregate at the present time because the aggregates are not sufficiently controllable and because the Bank can conceive of probable situations (for example, the instability of money demand) where it would not be optimal. However, because of the indicator properties of the monetary aggregates, the Bank does get concerned when they grow too quickly or too slowly.[10]

Howitt notes that "the important idea that a central bank, or more generally a government, could act as a focal point to help the economy select a good rational-expectations equilibrium in the case of multiple equilibria is an extremely important message.... We understand too little about what makes some announcements credible and others not to dismiss the idea entirely." In a general sense credibility involves to a greater or lesser extent the public's belief about all the parameters of the loss function used by the Bank. That is, if everyone knew that the Bank would act as if it had a high a and that it was the deviation of inflation (p) from zero, not four percent that mattered, our job would be easier. The bank does not pretend that it has credibility (in the technical sense), but it knows that its job would indeed be easier if it did. In the meantime, life goes on and since inflation is the growth in a nominal variable, the Bank continues to be concerned with the growth of nominal variables such as nominal spending, monetary and credit aggregates and wages.[11]

NOTES

1 Both Coyne and the mainstream of the 1950s differ considerably from the current mainstream based on extensions of the pioneering work of Mundell and Fleming.

2 Since the Minister of Finance was given the power to issue a directive to the Bank with respect to monetary policy, he must take ultimate responsibility for that policy. However, the fact that the Bank operates with a large measure of independence also means that as long as no directive is in effect, the Bank must also bear that responsibility.

3 In his presentation, Howitt noted that his model was only one of several that one could use to analyze the Bank of Canada's behaviour.

4 To be complete, rational-expectations models need to describe the costs of information and how the model is to be learned.

5 In an ideal world the central bank would have developed at its inception (time t=0) the ideal loss function as a function of v_t and kept it constant forever. But central banks need to learn too. The Bank of Canada has drawn a lesson about the results of not acting in a sufficiently timely fashion from the experience of the inflation in the 1970s. As a result the speed of the policy response to inflationary concerns has changed. In effect, the result is as if a has risen and p'_t has fallen. Furthermore, v_t has risen because of a variety of institutional and demographic changes. See D. Rose (1988).

6 The Bank of Canada, like most central banks and governments, has no explicit loss function that one can write down as a mathematical formula. The discussion here describes central bank behaviour as if it were derived from an explicit loss function.

7 Given the accountability of the central bank, it is not surprising that it attempts to explain what it would like to see happen.

8 Given his beauty contest example, Keynes would not likely have accepted strong forms of rational expectations. Therefore, it is not unKeynesian for a central bank to assume that private agents do not always follow strong forms of rational expectations with rigidly given models.

9 In loss function terms, Howitt appears to be arguing for $(u-v)^2 + ap^2$, where a is large.

[10]　On the indicator properties of the monetary aggregates see Hostland, Poloz, and Storer (1987).

[11]　See, in particular, Crow (1988).

REFERENCES

Crow, J.W. "The Work of Canadian Monetary Policy: Eric J. Hanson Memorial Lecture" *Bank of Canada Review*, June, 1988.

Gordon, H. Scott (1961) *The Economists versus the Bank of Canada*, Toronto: Ryerson Press.

Hostland, D.; Poloz, S.; and Storer, P. "An Analysis of the Information Content of Alternative Credit Aggregates," *Bank of Canada Technical Report* 48, 1987.

Newman, Peter C. *Renegade in Power: The Diefenbaker Years*, Toronto: McClelland and Stewart, 1963.

Rose, David "The NAIRU in Canada: Concepts, determinants and estimates," *Bank of Canada Technical Report*, 50, 1988.

E52
E58 *126*
E12
E13

Canada
p 95: Comments   126 - 32

NICHOLAS ROWE

RULES RESTORED

As usual, Peter Howitt's paper is an excellent example of scholarship —
balanced, well-reasoned, clearly presented, and furthermore too modest
about its own contribution. Its central message is, however, quite wrong.

I am going to do three things. First, I will restate what I take to be
Peter's central point — that rules are impossible. Second, I will
demonstrate that his central point is empirically false — rules cannot be
impossible for they are in fact (sometimes) observed. Third, I will try to
explain *why* it is that rational people (sometimes) follow rules rather than
discretion, and are trusted to do so.

RESTATING PETER HOWITT'S CENTRAL POINT

The game between the central bank and the public can be represented as
follows:

Public

Bank	Expect Rules	Expect Discretion
Follow Rules	2nd	4th
Follow Discretion	1st	3rd

The four cells are ranked according to the bank's preferences, which
may (but need not) also represent social welfare. The ranking of outcomes
follows Kydland and Prescott (1977) and is not here at issue.

What is the equilibrium? First, note that given rational expectations,
the public will expect the bank to follow the policy it actually does follow, eliminating the first and fourth ranked outcome as equilibria. Kydland and Prescott's point is then that the second best outcome under rules
is better than the third best outcome under discretion, thus the bank should
choose rules. But Peter replies that whether the public expects rules or
expects discretion, the bank always does better by choosing discretion,
which is thus the dominant strategy, so eliminating the second and fourth

ranked outcomes. The restrictions of rational expectations and dominant strategies together thus leave only the third ranked outcome as an equilibrium; the bank follows discretion and the public expects it to do so.

It is important to realize that Peter is *not* (at least not here) disputing Kydland and Prescott's argument that a credible rule would be *better* than anticipated discretion. Rather, he is arguing that a credible rule is *impossible.* If the bank could, by following a rule, get the public to expect the rule, it should do so. But it *cannot* get the public to expect anything other than discretion, and it should therefore choose discretion.

CREDIBLE RULES ARE NOT IN FACT IMPOSSIBLE

Peter argues that, at least under the present constitution, there is no way for the Bank of Canada to construct some external enforcement mechanism which could force it to stick to some pre-announced policy rule and so ensure the credibility of its commitment.

As an individual, I can construct an external enforcement mechanism for my own commitments by signing a legally binding contract. My following a rule can be enforced by the courts, and lower courts in turn are perhaps subject to enforcement by the Supreme Court, but then who or what is the external enforcement mechanism which ensures that the Supreme Court follows rules? *Quis custodiet eo ipso custodes?* In aggregate there exists no Leviathan or other *deus ex machina* to enforce our commitments to follow rules — and yet in many cases we do in fact follow rules and are confidently expected to do so.[1]

To see this, consider the following game between a magistrate (personifying the judicial system) and a (potential) criminal.

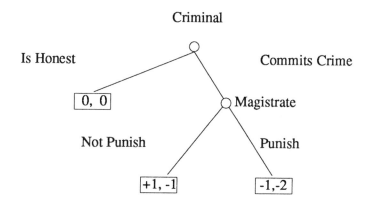

Criminal

Is Honest

Commits Crime

0, 0

Magistrate

Not Punish

Punish

+1, -1

-1,-2

The first figure represents the criminal's payoff and the second the magistrate's payoff. What is the equilibrium? Suppose the criminal does commit the crime. Will the magistrate punish him? Punishment, particularly when it takes the form of imprisonment rather than fines, as it often does, is very costly to society (especially if the criminal's utility is included, as it should be) and so a magistrate who cares about social welfare would choose not to punish. The criminal knows this, and so chooses to commit crime, since he gets higher pay-offs from getting away with crime than by being honest. Thus crime is never punished and is thus never deterred!

Just try to imagine a magistrate duped by Bellman's Principle of Optimality into a purely discretionary policy: "Now, I see you're charged with murder. How unfortunate; but it's no use crying over spilled milk. Bygones are forever bygones. No sense in making things worse by punishing you. Please don't do it again. Case dismissed!"

Now, the reader may object to the above that I have ignored one of the beneficial consequences of punishing criminals — that of deterring future crime — and that once the pay-offs to deterrence were included the magistrate would rationally punish the criminal. And I quite agree that it is indeed rational to punish to deter crime. But it is not the magistrate's *act* of punishment which deters crime — it is his being known to *follow a rule* of punishing criminals which deters crime. The particular act of punishing this criminal cannot prevent the crime he has already committed, and matters only as an enforcement of the rule of punishing criminals — an act whose performance is necessary to uphold the magistrate's reputation for following this rule. To all this I agree, but in justifying the rationality of punishment in this way we admit exactly what is at issue — that it is rational to follow rules and that magistrates do in fact follow them and are confidently expected to do so.

As a matter of empirical fact, Bellman's Principle of Optimality overwhelmingly fails to hold. People do *not* always let bygones be bygones. They do *not* always follow discretion, but instead frequently follow rules, and are expected to do so. They *do* pay debts and honour contracts, thereby recognizing the importance of bygone promises. If they did not thus follow rules, open market operations, for instance would be meaningless, and the Bank of Canada itself, as an institution defined by a set of contractual and legal relations, could not logically exist.

Whatever actually exists cannot be impossible, and so it is not impossible to follow a rule and be expected to do so.

Just a couple of blocks from the Bank of Canada lies the Supreme Court. It too is merely a stone and glass building with a green copper roof populated with men and women of varying intelligence, education, and moral character. Each has a high degree of autonomy from the government of the day. I can see no *a priori* reason why it should be any less possible for the Bank of Canada to follow rules than it is for the Supreme Court.

EXPLAINING WHY RATIONAL PEOPLE CHOOSE TO FOLLOW RULES

I will now try to reconcile the *fact* of rule-following with the *theory* of rational behaviour. In stating my task in that way I hope I make it clear exactly what is at stake should my attempted reconciliation fail. Rule-following is *not* at stake; it is an observed fact. If the reader does not accept my attempt to explain why it is rational to follow rules, and believes that no such attempt can succeed, it is not the fact of rule-following but rather the theory of rational behaviour which he must then jettison.

From a positive pespective, if it is not rational to follow rules then we must accept that people are not in fact rational. And from a normative perspective, if the general acceptance and adoption of a consequentialist ethical theory, (the act-utilitarianism for instance) leads to bad consequences then, as noted by Hodgson (1967), that is an argument against a consequentialist and in favour of a deontological ethical theory (like rule-utilitarianism for instance).

Peter Howitt notes that his argument against rules "... rests on the simple observation that if the bank is going to act rationally, then people will be able to calculate for themselves what the bank's reaction function will be. Thus they will be able correctly to forecast the bank's instrument setting, contingent upon the realization of the wage-shock, independently of anything that the bank actually says or does. If the bank were to contemplate deviating from the equilibrium setting of its instrument this period there is no way that such a departure could influence those expectations, which have been calculated on the basis of people's rational expectations."

In Rowe (1989) I call this the Axiom of Decidability. It is the claim that, given the requisite knowledge of a person's underlying preferences and information, his rational choices can in principle be perfectly predicted (up to a purely random component when he is perfectly indifferent between alternatives). Given the Axiom of Decidability, the rest of Peter's argument follows logically. That axiom, however, I claim is false.

It is not possible even in principle to predict a person's rational choices *a priori independently of his wanting you to be able to predict them a priori.*

Suppose the Decidability Axiom were true. If it is, logic inexorably leads to the conclusion that discretion rather than rules is rational, people expect this, and the outcome is the third best. Suppose on the other hand that the Decidability Axiom were false. Being unable to predict the bank's behaviour *a priori*, people would need to predict it *a posteriori*, on the basis of their observations of the bank's actual past behaviour. And if they form their expectations this way, it may be rational for the bank to create a reputation for following a rule, and thus attain the second best outcome. Preferring the second best to the third best, the bank would prefer the Decidability Axiom to be false. How can it make it false? Simply by following a rule, for we have already seen that the Decidability Axiom logically entails discretion, so by negating discretion the bank negates the Decidability Axiom by *modus tollens*. Thus the bank chooses to falsify the Decidability Axiom, so it is indeed false, and reputation and rules are indeed possible.

In his Section 5, Peter Howitt asks whether we could ever get a reputational equilibrium in which the bank sticks to its rule because it knows that breaking the rule would cause people to expect discretion thereafter. He doubts that we could get such an equilibrium, for it is hard to explain how the public could come to have the required expectational mechanism-expecting rules if rules have been observed in the past, but discretion otherwise. I would counter that the very disagreement between us illustrates how such expectations could arise. Either Howitt is right, and credible rules are impossible, or else Rowe is right, and they are possible. If the bank thinks Howitt is right it will choose discretion now and in the future. (And if it realizes that the public will realize this, the bank will rationally choose rules, which proves that Rowe is indeed right!)

In Section 6 he examines the possibility of reputation when the public does not know *a priori* the bank's underlying preferences. I interpret his answer to be that reputation is possible in this instance, but that the bank's optimal (perfect equilibrium) policy is nevertheless discretionary (conforming to Bellman's Principle), and the wage equation is structural and based on adaptive expectations.

I will remark in passing that there is nothing *necessarily* irrational about adaptive expectations. The rational expectations hypothesis does not contradict simple expectations formation mechanisms as such — rather it contradicts the idea that any *one* such mechanism can be valid regardless of the circumstances. Rational expectations requires that the mechanism generating expectations match, both qualitatively and quantitatively, the actual statistical relationship between the variables in the information set and those to be forecast.

Returning to the main point, Peter's demonstration that the optimal policy is discretionary in this example really begs the question. He assumes that the public will use its noisy observation of the bank's actions to make inferences about the bank's preferences by calculating what choices the bank would make under various preferences *if the bank's choice were purely discretionary*. The public never contemplates the possibility that the bank will throw away its manual of optimal control theory and simply pick the Kydland and Prescott solution. If the public simply disbelieves the Axiom of Decidability (as it should), it can allow a non-zero prior possibility that the bank will follow rules rather than discretion, and can then interpret low observed inflation as due *either* to a preference for low inflation *or* to a bank that has chosen to follow a rule. And given that the public contemplates a possibility of rule-following, rules may be optimal.

In Section 7 Peter asks what would happen if the bank simply ignored this advice and "irrationally" followed a rule. He argues that nevertheless the bank will sooner or later see reason and restore discretion, and builds a model in which the public knows the per-period probability it will do so. I would like to make his model symmetrical, by adding a per-period probability that a discretionary bank will see *my* "reason" and switch back to rules once again. Academic economists do not generally have the immediate ear of the Governor of the Bank of Canada and the ability to set day-to-day policy in silent conspiracy. We do (perhaps) have the ability to slowly modify the prevailing intellectual climate concerning the conduct of policy, but in doing so we influence public expectations of policy as much and as quickly as we influence policy itself. What Peter is then doing by persuasively arguing for discretion rather than rules can be portrayed in his model as increasing the probability of switching from rules to discretion and reducing the probability of switching from discretion to rules. I can be portrayed as trying to do exactly the opposite. I conjecture[2] that the average present value of the bank's loss is increasing in the parameters Peter is increasing, and decreasing in the parameters I am (I hope) increasing, and vice versa, which, if verified, would prove (once again) that I am right and he is wrong! I also conjecture that the loss *might* (i.e. will for some parameter values) nevertheless be greater during times when my advice prevails than when his advice prevails (loosely, rules advocates save up credibility which discretion advocates then consume), which might lead an unwary econometrician to say that discretion is better than rules, thus perfectly illustrating the Lucas (1976) critique of econometric policy evaluation!

CONCLUSION

What Peter Howitt has shown is that economists have been insufficiently critical in their acceptance of the desirability of rules rather than discretion. Accepting the rationality of following rules requires rejecting what I call the Axiom of Decidability — that rational choice is in principle predictable — which many economists may not easily reject. But people do in fact follow rules, and we either reject decidability, or else reject the assumption that human behaviour is rational — which those same economists will even less easily reject.

NOTES

1   In Rowe (1989) I set out at much greater length my view that social institutions like property rights can only be understood as constituted by rule-following behaviour, and that it is indeed rational to follow rules.

2   I do not attempt to corroborate or falsify my conjecture here, so that subsequent calculations may independably test my intuition on these questions. Also I am slow at maths and rather lazy.

REFERENCES

Hodgson, D.H. *The Consequences of Utilitarianism, Clarendon Press, Oxford, 1967.*

Howitt, P.W. "Keynesian Policy Analysis, Rational Expectations, and the Bank of Canada," 1988.

Kydland, F.E. and E.C. Prescott "Rules Rather than Discretion: The Inconsistency of Optimal Plans" *Journal of Political Economy*, vol. 85, no. 3, 1977

Lucas, R.E. "Econometric Policy Evaluation: A Critique" in *The Phillips Curve and Labor Markets*, edited by K. Brunner and A.M. Melzer, Amsterdam: North-Holland, 1976.

Rowe, N. *Rules and Institutions*, Deddington, Oxford: Philip Allan, 1989.

Chapter VI

THE CASE FOR A DISCRETIONARY, POLITICALLY RESPONSIBLE CENTRAL BANK

Thomas K. Rymes*, Carleton University

In the early 1960s, H. Scott Gordon took part in a controversy about the Governor of the Bank of Canada, Mr. James Coyne. Professor Gordon's writings surrounding the controversy spanned a number of issues, ranging all the way from criticism of the Bank's misuse of money supply statistics designed to mask, in response to adverse public criticism, its implementation of "tight" monetary policy in the late 1950s,[1] a wonderfully polemical pamphlet setting out the reasons why a number of Canadian academic economists had been so unusually unanimous in writing the Minister of Finance calling for a change in the monetary policy and the management of the Bank of Canada,[2] to an academic discussion of the constitutional position of the Bank of Canada.[3]

In these works Professor Gordon dealt with a number of problems associated with central banking in a democratic market economy, not all of which I can deal with in this paper.

* This paper is written in honour of Professor H. Scott Gordon for the role he played in founding the Department of Economics at Carleton University in 1948 and his many contributions to economics. I should like to record my indebtedness particularly to Jack Galbraith for many discussions about banking and monetary problems and to Nicholas Rowe for his comments and the benefits I obtained from reading his *Rules and Institutions* (Deddington Oxford: Philip Allan, and Ann Arbor: University of Michigan Press, 1989).

The Bank's misuse of statistics lends credence to the bureaucratic theory of central banking which predicts that central banks will try to obfuscate the measures by which their conduct of monetary policy can be assessed and monitored, so blunting any effective criticism which can be made of their behaviour.[4] The adoption of monetary targeting by the Bank in 1975 would suggest, however, that it was prepared to see the success or failure of its policy judged by the movement of a particular measure no more subject to error, perhaps, than any other in economics. The early enthusiasm with which the Bank embraced targeting[6] was tempered by experience[7] but it is not clear whether monetary targeting is consistent with the view that a central bank has an incentive to obscure measures of its performance or whether central banks believed that the demand functions for money were so stable that indeed monetary targeting would be an excellent monitoring device by which the Bank would get high marks for performance even though successful targeting might not have any significant consequence as far as the macroeconomic performance of the economy was concerned.

The criticisms mounted against the monetary policy of the Bank of Canada by Professor Gordon in his pamphlet do *not* sound like criticisms today. Rather they sound like backhanded compliments. Consider these quotations from Chapter Four of *The Economists Versus The Bank of Canada.*

> One must keep the economic situation constantly under review and be prepared to shift the gears from forward to reverse and back again as the requirements of the economy alter. (13)

> Various statements by the present Governor of the Bank indicate that the doctrinaire anti-inflationism of the Bank is very deeply entrenched. The Governor has expressed the view, for example, that we must not expect monetary policy to do very much about the problem of unemployment. (14)

and

> The Governor of the Bank of Canada does not merely believe that inflation is an economic evil. He regards it as a moral wickedness that is utterly to be condemned and brooks no compromise. (14)

Few economists, nowadays, would be in favour of "fine tuning." Few would believe that money is nonneutral so that expected changes in the stock of money could effect the volume of employment. Most would accept the idea of supernonneutrality, which entails substantial welfare costs associated with inflation brought about by a policy linked not with expected changes in the level of the money supply but with its expected rate of growth. Attempts to engage in the discretionary monetary policy Professor Gordon was castigating the Bank of Canada for *not* following will not, it is now argued, have any effects on any "real" variables in the economy and will result merely in welfare losses associated with sustained inflation. Professor Gordon was writing before Friedman's American Economics Association presidential address,[7] the advent of the rational-expectations revolution and problem of time-inconsistency in monetary policy.

Professor Gordon also argued (Gordon 1961b, 1) that the "...constitutional status of the Bank, as it currently seems to be, is a gross incongruity in a parliamentary democracy based on the principle of executive responsibility."

The later understanding, arrived at when Mr. Rasminsky became Governor, that, in the advent of a disagreement between the Governor and the Minister of Finance, the Governor would have either to accede to a detailed directive regarding monetary policy, published by the Minister in *The Canada Gazette*, or resign, still does not resolve the issue raised by Professor Gordon of the joint responsibility for monetary policy now being shared by the Minister and the Governor of the Bank. I interpret Professor Gordon to suggest that the Bank of Canada should not have the independence, even if limited, it has now following the Rasminsky "Directive" understanding and that monetary policy should be conducted by a Department of Monetary Affairs. Such a recommendation is contrary to much of the literature today on central banking and monetary policy which it is suggested that such policy should be as free as possible from the entanglements of day-to-day political strife and indeed should be entrenched in rules in constitutional arrangements[8] or that, even further, one should get rid of central banks altogether.

I should argue that a central bank should be a Department of Monetary Affairs no different than (say) the Ministry of Finance in our parliamentary democracy in Canada. I shall, however, review the literature which arrives at sharply opposed conclusions and recommendations. The question which I am beginning to try to answer in this paper[9] is why is Professor Gordon's suggestion so much out of fashion today.

NEOCLASSICAL MONETARY THEORY

Consider the optimal neoclassical monetary growth literature.[10] Stemming from that theory, we may consider two portfolio equations

$$q_k \, (k, m) - (d + n + n' + p \,) = \eta \dot{c}/c$$

and

$$q_m \, (k, m) + i - p - (d_m + n + n' + p \,) = \eta \dot{c}/c$$

where q_k is the gross marginal physical product of capital, a negative function of the amount of capital for each Harrod person[11] input and a positive function of "real" fiat money balances for each Harrod person, q_m is the gross marginal physical product of the services of the "real" money balances, d is the rate of carrying cost or depreciation on real capital, d_m is the rate of carrying costs or service charge which holders and users of the services of "real" money balances pay the Authorities, *p* is the rate of time preference, i is the nominal rate of interest the Authorities pay on fiat money balances, p is the perfectly anticipated rate of inflation, c/c is the rate of growth of consumption of the Harrod agent and η is the elasticity of the marginal utility of consumption.[12]

At the steady state values of the equations when $\dot{c}/c$ is equal to zero, there will exist a k and an m (k_s, m_s) such that the net marginal product of capital, q_k - d, equals the steady state real rate of return, n + n' + *p*, and the net marginal physical product of money, q_m - d_m, *plus the real rate of interest being earned on money balances, i - p*, also equals the steady state rate of return. Once-over changes in the nominal money supply DO NOT have real effects while changes in the "real" rate of interest the Authorities arrange to be earned on money balances DO have real effects.

Consider the steady state solution. A once-over change in the costless fiat nominal money supply is associated with an equi-proportional change in the overall level of prices so that m, which is equal to $M/PL(0)e^{(n+n')t}$, is unchanged because the change in M is matched proportionally by the change in P. This standard neutrality proposition of the classical quantity theory of money holds by virtue of such assumptions as perfect price flexibility, clearing markets and the steady state.[13] Consider, however, a difference in the "real" rate of interest the Authorities pay on fiat money balances.[14] Suppose that the Authorities, by the lump-sum transfer route, pursue a rate of monetary expansion which is inflationary so that, while the nominal rate of interest on money balances remains unchanged, prices are now confidently expected to be rising at some positive rate. Consequently, the "real" rate of interest earned from holding money balances is lower, the demand for money balances will be reduced, the demand to hold commodities will be increased and there will be a higher temporary equilibrium price level such that "real" fiat money balances will be lower, the net marginal physical product of money balances will be higher offsetting to some extent the lower "real" rate of interest on money and the net marginal product of capital will also be lower. The case is illustrated in Figure 1.

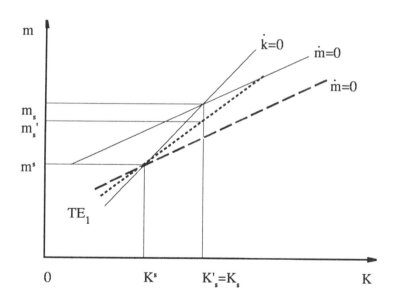

Figure 1

In Figure 1, the steady state combinations of real money balances and capital stocks which bring about the steady state rate of return to money balances and capital so that neither real money balances nor capital in Harrod units are growing, are designated respectively as $\dot{m} = 0$ and $\dot{k} = 0$. The steady state portfolio equilibrium conditions are given by the pair (m_s, k_s). The $\dot{m} = 0$ schedule is drawn up, however, for a particular "real" rate of interest, deemed to be under their control, paid on nominal fiat money balances by the Authorities. If the Authorities should impose a lower "real" rate of interest, that is, should they levy an inflationary tax, then a new $\dot{m} = 0$ schedule, the dashed line in Figure 1, is relevant. If one were at the original steady state, then, attempts to get out of money balances in response to the inflation tax levied by the Authorities would cause a higher temporary equilibrium price level such that a temporary portfolio equilibrium would prevail with "real" balances equal to m_s.[1] The real rates of return to money balances and capital are below their steady state levels and a process of decumulation and a sequence of ever higher temporary equilibrium price levels will occur until the economy is in a new steady state designated in Figure 1 by the pair (m_s, k_s). The Authorities, by varying the "real" rate of interest paid on money by (say) varying the rate of growth of the fiat money supply, are able to effect different steady states and supernonneutrality results. Such supernonneutrality is the source of all the "inflation tax" literature and welfare loss calculations associated with steady inflation.

SIGNIFICANCE OF THE ROLE OF THE CENTRAL BANK

It is the failure of the Authorities to pay a "real" rate of interest on costless fiat money, equal to the steady state real rate of return, which is the "inflation" tax and the source of the nonoptimality of the monetary arrangements associated with fiat money. **It is a very peculiar result.**

The Authorities are providing a service which is obtained by the holding and use of fiat money balances and which I have suggested is efficiently priced by the carrying cost or *service charge*. If the service charge is efficient, then it should metre or measure the value of the marginal product of the otherwise costless provision of the services of fiat money balances. That is, the net marginal product of the service of the "real" fiat money balances should be zero.[15] If the fiat money balances are also a part of wealth, then, in the steady state, they should be earning the steady state rate of return. If the Authorities pay the steady state rate of return as the "real" rate of interest on money balances, then the price level will be such that real money balances and capital stocks will be such that the services of "real" fiat money balances will be efficiently priced, that is, $q_m(m, k) - d_m = 0$. The whole question boils down, then, to the failure of the Authorities to ensure that fiat money balances earn a "real" rate of interest on fiat money which equals the steady state rate of return. What role is there for the Monetary Authorities in such analysis? Since it is assumed that the only service being provided by the Authorities, the transaction service in the form of clearing arrangements,[16] is competitively priced, it would surely follow that, in terms of the portfolio service which money performs with capital as components of wealth, competition would ensure that the portfolio service of money would be privately produced and money would earn a "real" rate of interest equal to the real rate of return being earned on capital. The point can be seen by assuming that the fiat money is reserves held by private banks behind their deposit liabilities. It is now a commonplace to recognize that required non-interest bearing cash reserves are a tax on the banking industry, really a tax on the provision of the transactions services of outside and, consequently, inside money. This tax will result in banks paying "real" interest rates on bank deposits less than the real rate of return earned on their loans and thus on the real capital of the economy and in service charges for the transactions services rendered by bank deposits being less than the marginal product of "real" bank deposits.[17] The Monetary Authorities may levy a service charge for the transactions services being provided to the banks by the reserves — a service charge which would mimic the competitive price for such services. But unless the Monetary Authorities were also allowing banks to determine the optimum amount of reserves and were paying the steady state real rate of return as the "real" interest rate on reserves held, the conditions of inefficient monetary arrangements would hold. If the banks were allowed to hold optimum reserves and if the transactions services being provided by the reserves (that is, by the Monetary Authorities) were competitively priced, then should the Authorities try to tax the banks by not paying the competitive real rate of return on reserves. The banks would then begin to develop their own reserves which would earn the competitive rate of return. The real rate of interest on outside money, if it continued to be used by the banks,[18] would be at the competitive level.[19] Putting the matter another way, optimum monetary arrangements would result if the Monetary Authorities paid on optimally held reserves a "real" rate of interest equal to the steady state rate of return.

The conclusion which follows immediately is that if the Monetary Authorities do not follow the optimum monetary policies they must be constrained to do so *OR* the Monetary Authorities must be wound up and replaced with private banking arrangements.[20] The Point of the argument so far is that these two conclusions are one and the same. Monetary Authorities constrained, perhaps even constitutionally constrained, to follow the optimum money supply policies of the neoclassical monetary growth theory literature are Monetary Authorities which could be supplanted by *laissez-faire* monetary arrangements without any real effects or welfare gains or losses. It is a long way from the recommendation that independent Monetary Authorities should become Departments of Monetary Affairs in parliamentary democracies, indeed, the argument so far would seem to be taking us in the opposite direction.

DISCRETIONARY POLICY

The reason why Monetary Authorities in charge of fiat monetary arrangements should be constrained to behave constitutionally by rules or can be replaced without cost by *laissez-faire* banking arrangements is that the Authorities have, it would appear, nothing to do.[21] Indeed, the argument is that discretionary Monetary Authorities, having no real role to play, if they try to play such a role, will have negative consequences in that they move the economy away from optimum monetary arrangements.

Consider again the first order conditions and the departure from the optimum conditions outlined in Figure 1. When the Authorities lowered the "real" rate of interest on fiat money balances, the initial temporary equilibrium where the price level rose entailed rates of return on money balances and capital below the steady state rate and a burst of consumption above the optimum rate of consumption the initial monetary arrangements would ensure. In the new steady state the consumption levels are reduced and it is the reduction in the consumption levels away from that associated with monetary optimality which is the welfare loss associated with the adoption of non-optimal arrangements by the Authorities. The Authorities might well do this, however, if they valued the short run gain in consumption achieved above the long run loss. Authorities which do this are imposing welfare costs on their community.[22] Such Authorities must be constrained from undertaking the discretionary act of altering the "real" rate of interest on fiat money balances. The Authorities might also come to believe that the benefits from a temporary increase in consumption obtained by "breaking the rule," that is, by not paying the monetary optimum "real" rate of interest on fiat money are worthwhile even if the departures cannot be too great because the loss in welfare becomes greater and greater, the greater the extent of the departure. Members of the community will, however, begin to form their expectations in terms of Monetary Authorities so consistently departing from optimality and the economy will settle into a non-optimal monetary arrangement equilibrium simply because the Authorities, with the freedom to behave in a discretionary way, are expected to depart from the optimum arrangements.[23] The Authorities, when pursuing the optimum rule, ensure that the community enjoys the monetary optimum level of consumption. When the Authorities depart, it is not because they expect the community to go on consuming at the old level, (rather, they know the community will respond to the rule revision), but because they value more highly than does the economy the initially higher levels of consumption along the sequence of temporary equilibria as the economy moves from the monetary optimum steady state to the non-optimum steady state. As a consequence, discretionary action by the Authorities comes to be anticipated by the members of the community and the steady state levels of consumption never rise to the monetary optimum level and the "real" rate of interest on fiat money settles at some non-optimum money supply policy level.

If Monetary Authorities are to be retained then they must be constrained to follow the optimum money supply rules. Time-inconsistency will lead the Authorities, acting in a discretionary way, and the community into a discretionary equilibrium which is inferior to that of the rule-governed monetary optimum equilibrium.

It would appear that the arguments against discretionary Monetary Authorities are indeed formidable. The arguments really amount to suggesting that the Authorities should be disbanded. It would appear that if Monetary Authorities are retained as an institutional form, whether or not they are a constitutionally constrained independent authority or whether they are a similarly constrained Ministry of Monetary Affairs, or even a division within the Department of Finance, would seem to be matters of little significance. If they are replaced by *laissez-faire* banking, then of course, the question of their independence from parliamentary democracy becomes otiose in the sense that they will be governed by no more nor no less than the usual *rules* of contract.

STABILITY

One fundamental assumption made in the all the foregoing neoclassical optimal monetary growth literature is that the economic system is stable. All markets are clearing in all temporary equilibria. The sequence of temporary equilibria terminates in a unique full or steady state equilibrium. It is the assumption of stability which yields such results as the Authorities have no real role to play, could be supplanted by *laissez-faire* banking arrangements and the fear that, if such Authorities are retained they will attempt to do "real" things and must be constrained from doing so. One must consider the possibility of instability. Since there is nothing in the basic framework of ideas which permits us to say that the economic system is inherently stable or unstable, one must at least consider the possibility of instability and even then only instability in the limited sense of saddlepoint instability.

In a monetary economy, there are three types of instability to examine. With respect to the "real" value of money balances, there is the possibility that "real" balances will not gravitate to steady state because the denominator, i.e. the price level, will not necessarily move to a steady state value even if the numerator, the stock of nominal money balances, behaves in a stable fashion. Second, there is the possibility that even if the price level were inherently stable, the stock of nominal money balances would not behave. That is, there may be the cases where, even with prices falling, the nominal stock of bank deposits might be falling even faster so that "real" bank deposits are falling — a situation which could be said to hold in the early 1930s in the USA. There is even the deeper possibility that instability in the movement of prices and nominal money may be such that Keynesian problems of insufficiency in aggregate demand will not necessarily be eliminated by "real" fiat money balance effects. The second problem falls under the general rubric of instability in private banking operations, such as bank runs, and is said to be reason why central banks, as bankers clubs, would exist.[24] The third possibility is beyond the scope of this paper. The first possibility has been one of concern to monetary theorists such as Wicksell and Keynes and is the one which I examine for illustrative purposes. The possibility arises because of myopic expectations or nonconstant returns to scale monetary technologies. Consistent with the use of rational expectations, I shall adopt the second possibility for investigation. It may be done with the aid of Figure 2.

Figure 2

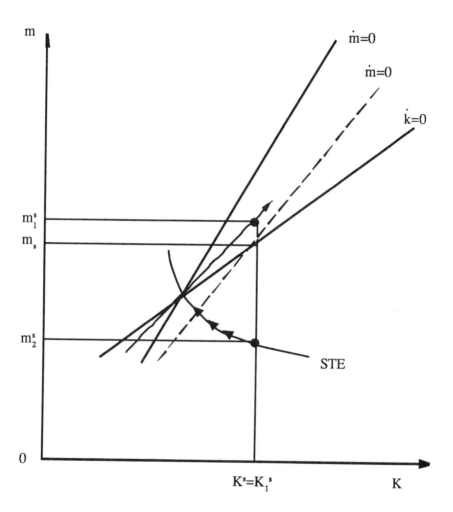

In Figure 2, the slopes of the two portfolio balance equations have been reversed, compared to Figure 1, indicating the monetary technology might be characterized by increasing returns to scale. Consider the consequences. Assume that the economy is in a sub-optimum monetary state exhibited by intersection of the two schedules yielding the steady state solutions m_s and k^s. Authorities then adopt the rule of paying on money balances a "real" rate of interest equal to the steady state rate of return. Initially, the new temporary equilibrium involves a lower price level, since the holding of money is now more attractive. The result however, is that now rates of return to money balances and capital are above the steady state $n + n' + \eta$. Accumulation of capital and "real" money balances are increasingly attractive and the economy is off on an explosive path of such accumulation, with lower and lower price levels or hyperdeflation. One can equally postulate any other real disturbance of the equilibrium such that the economy, seeking to hold smaller and smaller stocks of capital and "real" money balances, is off on a program of hyperinflation. There is, however, a stable temporary equilibrium. The members of the economy expect Monetary Authorities to prevent such monetary instability. In the example discussed, the Authorities must realize that the problem is that the expected rate of return on holding money is too *high*, the members of the economy rationally expect that the Authorities will at some time lower the "real" rate of interest on money balances in a discretionary way such that the holding of money balances is made less, not more, attractive and as a consequence the temporary equilibrium price level is such that m^s_2 are the initial money balances held. The economy then follows the course depicted in Figure 2 by STE, the locus of the temporary equilibria, the sequence of which leads the economy to the steady state equilibrium at which the optimum money supply rules hold. The point of the argument, however, is this: To ensure the steady state equilibria, the Authorities must pursue a sequence of discretionary "real" rates of interest on money balances. If the Authorities followed an optimum money supply rule, the economy would exhibit instability. If the Authorities practice discretion, the problem of instability *may* be overcome. A role for discretionary Monetary Authorities exists in that members of the community confidently expect the Authorities to behave in a discretionary manner to preserve stability in the value of money.[25] I do not want to understate the difficulties the Authorities face since along the Stable Temporary Equilibrium locus, it will be necessary for the Authorities to be continually revising the "real" rate of interest on money the community expects them to pay in order to ensure stability.[26]

The nature of the problem has now been altered. When stability of a monetary economy was assumed, there was no role for Monetary Authorities in that *laissez-faire* banking would do just as well. Monetary Authorities constrained constitutionally to follow optimum money supply policy rules would, in fact, mimic competitive private banking arrangements so that one could get rid of the Authorities. If it were considered impossible to get rid of them then they should be constrained from discretionary policy because such discretion is predicted to make the community worse off. In terms of Pareto efficiency, rule-constrained Authorities and *laissez-faire* Monetary Arrangements are identical. Once instability is considered possible, then a discretionary role for the Authorities can be considered. The problem is, however, that no one can be sure what situation the economy is in. If it is stable, then one would want rule-constrained Authorities or no Authorities at all. If instability prevails, then discretion by the Authorities is required.

POLITICALLY RESPONSIBLE DISCRETIONARY AUTHORITIES

Some of those who have argued that Monetary Authorities should be subject to constitutional rules nevertheless argue that, in a democracy, such Authorities should not be independent but should be part of normal government departments.[27] The essence of stability is predictability in the "real" value of the money supply, that is, one could imagine stationary or steady declines in the overall price level provided optimum "real" rates of interest are paid on money. (I assume that one is not going to accept some commodity money to achieve such stability since the costlessness of *stable*[28] fiat money, whether publicly or privately produced, will always swamp commodity monies even if such commodity monies seemed always to assure stability in the general price level.[29]) With stability assumed, it might be thought that an independent unconstrained Monetary Authority has an incentive to invest in its reputation of preserving such monetary stability even though as we have seen such Authorities might conceive of gaining from discretionary action by breaking such rules. If one assumes stability, however, I see no reason for Monetary Authorities, constitutionally constrained or otherwise, to exist. If one assumes instability then one must have discretion. Why should any discretionary monetary policy be in the hands — even partially — of an independent Authority? Is there any reason to argue that independent Monetary Authorities know better when discretion is required and when rules should be followed? Even a quasi-independent Monetary Authority could evolve into a bureaucracy unresponsive and not responsible to the general interests of society, which, in the presence of doubt about whether the monetary system is or is not stable, is something which cannot be ascertained independently of the democratic political process.[30] It is the unresolvable doubt about whether the monetary system is stable or unstable, even in the narrow sense set out in this paper, which means that discretion and parliamentary debate are inescapable. In a democracy, I can see no reason why monetary policy should not be the responsibility of the Department of Monetary Affairs, subject to the same controls exercised by the people in a parliamentary democracy. The Department would be responsible for both the conduct of policy and the policy itself. We have at present in Canada the argument that the bank is responsible for the conduct of policy and is jointly responsible for the policy though in the last analysis the Minister of Finance, the government and Parliament are responsible for the policy. I see no reason whatsoever why the Bank of Canada should be responsible, even jointly, for monetary policy. Short of the written directive under the Rasminsky understanding, with the Bank of Canada said sometimes to be responsible to Parliament, there is always ambiguity as to whether the government or the Bank of Canada is responsible for monetary policy. To close with a quote from Professor Gordon, the only argument I can see against a discretionary, politically responsible Department of Monetary Affairs is "...a distressing and debilitating distrust of the essential political process of democratic government." (Gordon, 1961b).

NOTES

[1] H.S. Gordon and L.N., Read "The political economics of the Bank of Canada," *Canadian Journal of Economics and Political Science,* XXIV, November 1958, pp. 465-82. (Hereinafter Gordon and Read).

[2] H. Scott Gordon, *The Economists Versus the Bank of Canada* (Toronto: Ryerson Press, 1961). Hereinafter Gordon 1961a).

[3] H.S. Gordon, "The Bank of Canada in a system of responsible government," *Canadian Journal of Economics and Political Science,* XXCII, February 1961, pp. 1-22. (Hereinafter Gordon 1961b). I do not want the hereinafter designations a and b to indicate which of the two pieces published by Professor Gordon in 1961 was written first.

[4] On the bureaucratic theory of central banking, see K. Acheson and J. Chant, "Bureaucratic theory and the choice of central bank goals." *Journal of Money, Credit, and Banking,* May 1973, pp. 637-55 reprinted in eds. E.F. Toma and M. Toma, *Central Bankers, Bureaucratic Incentives, and Monetary Policy* (Dordrecht: Martinus Nijhoff, 1986) and K. Acheson, "Bureaucratic theory: retrospect and prospect," eds. A. Breton *et al, European Journal of Political Economy,* Extra Issue, IV, 1988, pp. 18-46.

[5] Freeman wrote that (191/12) "On the whole we have been successful so far in keeping the trend rate of increase of the money stock broadly in line with our successive targets." and (192) "...the practice of monetary targeting is still very much alive and well in Canada." See G.E. Freeman, "A central banker's view of targeting," ed. Brian Griffiths and Geoffrey E. Wood, *Monetary Targets,* (Hong Kong: Macmillan, 1981).

[6] By the year in which Freeman's paper was published, the Bank had in fact abandoned formal targeting. As Thiessen stated in early 1982 the problems associated with targeting (16) "...will make it difficult to indicate a specific target path for M_1 for the time being." Gordon G. Thiessen, "The Canadian experience with monetary targeting," a paper given at the International Conference on *Monetary Targeting,* May 1982.

[7] Milton Friedman, "The role of monetary policy," *American Economic Review,* LVIII, March 1968, pp. 1-17 reprinted in ed. K.R. Leube, *The Essence of Friedman* (Stanford University, California: Hoover Institution Press, 1987).

8   See ed. L.B. Yeager, *In Search of a Monetary Constitution* (Cambridge, Mass: Harvard University Press, 1962) and Geoffrey Brennan and James M. Buchanan, *The Reason of Rules: Constitutional Political Economy* (Cambridge: Cambridge University Press, 1985).

9   For preliminary attempts to see why a discretionary Monetary Authority may be necessary, see T.K. Rymes, "Keynes and Stable Money," eds. *Keynes and Public Policy After Fifty Years, II, Theories and Method* (Aldershott; Edward Elgar, 1988) and "On the publicness of fiat money," eds. A. Asimakopulos *et al*, *Economic Theory, Welfare and the State* (London: Macmillan, forthcoming).

10   For statements of such literature see, for example, R. Dornbusch and J.A. Frenkel, "Inflation and growth: alternative approaches," *Journal of Money, Credit and Banking*, V, February 1973, pp. 141-156 and Stanley Fischer, "A framework for monetary and banking analysis," *Economic Journal*, Conference Papers 1983, pp. 1-16.

11   A Harrod "person" is one whose willingness to work, that is, each individual's supply of labour, and whose willingness to save, that is, each individual's supply of waiting resulting in his/her holdings of capital, are augmented by the latest technology. As a consequence, the number of natural individuals in the economy is growing at the rate n and the number of Harrod augmented persons in the economy is growing at the rate n + n' where n' is the rate of Harrod-neutral technical progress.

12   For similar equations, see "The essential properties of interest and money," Chapter 17 in J.M. Keynes, *The General Theory of Employment, Interest and Money: The Collected Writings of John Maynard Keynes* (Cambridge: Macmillan for the Royal Economic Society, 1973.

13   Lucas argues (S402) "Technically, I think of economics as studying decision rules that are steady states of some adaptative process, decision rules that are found to work over a range of situations and hence are no longer revised appreciably as more experience accumulates," Robert E. Lucas, Jr., "Adaptive behaviour and economic theory," *Journal of Business*, LIX, October 1986, S 410-426.

14   There is an important question as to the feasibility of the operation the Authorities are assumed to be able to perform. The Authorities might well be paying a nominal rate of interest on money balances

which equals the Harrod natural rate of growth. In that case the steady state rate of inflation would be equal to zero if the interest payments were the only source of monetary growth. The Authorities might be deemed to be in possession of a lump-sum transfer/tax mechanism (helicopters or furnaces) which would permit them to expand the money supply at a faster rate. If the lump-sum transfer were expressed in terms of a proportional rate of growth of the money stock, x, then the steady state rate of change of prices would be $p = (i + x) - (n + n')$, that is, $p > 0$. It is assumed that such lump-sum transfer/taxes exist so that the operation, by which the Authorities can alter the "real" rate of interest paid on money balances, is feasible. For doubts about such feasibility, see T.K. Rymes, "The logical impossibility of optimum money supply rules, *Carleton Economic Papers*, pp. 72-15; John Harkness, "The neutrality of money in neoclassical growth models," *Canadian Journal of Economics*, XI, November 1978, pp. 701-13; and John N. Smithin, "A note on the welfare cost of perfectly anticipated inflation," *Bulletin of Economic Research*, XXXV, May 1983, pp. 65-69.

[15] It will be noticed that the net marginal product of capital is not zero. Capital and its service flow are not costless. A unit of consumption must be given up to acquire a unit of capital. The service flow of the capital good is acquired only by surrendering a permanent stream of consumption which, for the Harrod agent, has a price of $n + n' + p$. Hence, in the steady state, one has $q_k (m, k) - d = n + n' + p$.

[16] Richard H. Timberlake, Jr., *The Origins of Central Banking in the United States* (Cambridge, Mass: Harvard University Press, 1978) and "The central banking role of clearinghouse associations," *Journal of Money, Credit, and Banking*, XVI, February 1984, pp. 1-15.

[17] For a statement of this result, see John J. Merrick, Jr. and Anthony Saunders, "Bank regulation and monetary policy," *Journal of Money, Credit, and Banking*, XVII, November 1985, pp. 691-117 and for a theoretical development of the argument, see Thomas K. Rymes, "The theory and measurement of the nominal output of banks, sectoral rates of saving and wealth in the National Accounts," eds. Robert Lipsey and Helen Stone Tice, *The Measurement of Saving, Investment and Wealth* (Chicago: University of Chicago Press for the NBER, Inc., 1989).

[18]   The Bank of Canada is abandoning legal cash reserves and so the
      "reserve tax," which is just another version of the inflation tax, is
      apparently being reduced. Under the new regulations being proposed,
      however, financial institutions directly involved in the daily clearing
      process (chartered banks and non-bank deposit-taking institutions) will
      be *required* to hold settlement clearing balances with the Bank, so
      that the "reserve tax" reappears in another guise. See Bank of Canada,
      "Discussion paper on the implementation of monetary policy in the
      absence of reserve requirements," (Ottawa, September 29, 1987) and
      "Second discussion paper on the implementation of monetary policy
      in a system with zero reserve requirements," (Ottawa, February 2,
      1989). See also David Longworth, "Optimal behaviour of direct
      clearers in a world with zero reserve requirements," a paper given to
      the Monetary Seminar in the Department of Economics at Carleton
      University, May 3, 1989.

[19]   Neil Wallace, "A suggestion for oversimplifying the theory of money,"
      Economic Journal, XCII, Conference 1988, pp. 25-36.

[20]   For the latest manifestations of this argument, see George Selgin, *The
      Theory of Free Banking: Money supply under competitive note issue.*
      (Totowa, N.J.: Rowman and Littlefield, 1988) and David Glasner,
      Free Banking and Monetary Reform (Cambridge: Cambridge Uni-
      versity Press, 1989).

[21]   This can be seen by imagining an economy in which the steady state
      rate of return would be $n + n'$, that is, the economy would be charac-
      terized by zero time preference. Then, Authorities following the op-
      timum money supply growth rule rather than paying the equivalent
      "real" rate of interest on fiat money would do nothing! Monetary Au-
      thorities with nothing to do are just another form of *laissez-faire*. The
      optimum money supply policy would be to fix the *level* of the nomi-
      nal stock of fiat money once over and then close up shop. In the steady
      state the rate of deflation would be equal to $n + n'$ and so the "real"
      rate of interest on fiat money, now appearing as a "real" capital gain
      rate, would be equal to the steady state rate of return and monetary
      arrangements would be efficient. If time preference exists, then, the
      capital gain rate would be less than the real rate of return and mon-
      etary arrangements would be suboptimal. Friedman has argued that
      the stock of nominal fiat money should be frozen with a zero growth
      rate, even if that is not the same rule as he earlier outlined in his "The

optimum quantity of money" because zero growth is a Schelling point. See M. Friedman, "The case for overhauling the Federal Reserve," *Challenge*, July-August 1985, pp. 4-15.

[22] Feldstein, employing the assumption of an expectations augmented Philips curve, has the Authorities lowering the rate of unemployment below the natural rate for some time by reducing the "real" rate of interest on fiat money balances. However, the welfare loss associated with such a lower rate eventually persuades the Authorities to return the rate to the monetary optimum level, resulting in some increase in the rate of unemployment above the natural rate for some time. The Authorities should not discriminate between generations of workers and, as a consequence, all its misguided discretionary policy manages to do is to impose the welfare costs of nonoptimal monetary arrangements on the economy for some finite time. Should the Authorities not reverse the non-optimality of the "real" interest rate on money, the welfare losses become very large indeed in his model, approaching infinity! See Martin Feldstein, "The welfare cost of permanent inflation and optimal short run economic policy," *Journal of Political Economy*, LXXXVI, August 1979, pp. 745-768.

[23] If one assumes an expectations augmented Philips curve, then the Authorities, while they should pursue the optimum "real" rate of interest on fiat money balances, will be tempted to reduce the attractiveness of holding money if there is a short run gain in employment. Again, assuming that the welfare losses associated with departures from the optimum rule are increasing with respect to the departures and that the members of the community come to expect the Authorities to depart from the rule, then the economy will settle at a non-optimum steady state at which any further discretionary departure by the Authorities from monetary rules, even if those rules are non-optimal, is eliminated by the costs of such departures. See Finn E. Kydland and Edward C. Prescott, "Rules rather than discretion: the inconsistency of optimal plans," *Journal of Political Economy*, LXXXV, June 1977, pp. 473-91 and R.J. Barro, "Recent developments in the theory of rules versus discretion," *Economic Journal*, XCVI, Conference Papers 1986, pp. 23-37. It is important to appreciate that policy by rule does not mean Authorities paying *unchanging* real rates of interest on fiat money balances. Each time $n + n' + \eta$ changes, the real rate set by the Authorities would change. On this point, see Bennett

T. McCallum, "The case for rules in the conduct of monetary policy: A concrete example," *Weltwirtschaftliches Archiv*, CXXIII, 1987, pp. 415-429.

[24] See C.A.E. Goodhart, "Why do banks need a central bank?," *Oxford Economic Papers*, XXXIX, January 1987, pp. 75-89 and extended in Chapter Seven of his *The Evolution of Central Banks* (Cambridge, Mass: The MIT Press, 1988).

[25] Rather than being a theoretical curiosum, the existence of saddlepoint instability under rational expectations provides credence both to the examination of such equilibria and to the possibility of discretionary action by Authorities. See Chapter 3 The rational expectations hypothesis in David. K.H. Begg, *The Rational Expectations Revolution in Macroeconomics* (Oxford: Philip Alan, 1982).

[26] There are two arguments in the literature that Authorities will contribute to instability or, with discretion, will behave in an unstable way. Selgin argues that, with monopoly note issue in the hands of the Authorities, the problem of internal drain will contribute to monetary instability in the inside component of the money supply. Increased demand by private banks for notes requires offsetting activities by the Authorities which may not occur if notes were privately produced and circulated by competitive banks. Selgin never discusses the ability of modern Monetary Authorities with monopoly note issue to offset such internal drains automatically through the movement of government deposits held with the Authorities and private banks. Friedman and Schwartz argue that the Federal Reserve failed to behave in a correct discretionary way in the early 1930s, indeed the effect of the failure on the money supply was even greater than if they had been following money supply rules, and this failure contributed to the instability of the monetary system.

[27] See Milton Friedman, "Should there be an independent monetary authority?" ed. L.B. Yeager, *op. cit.* and his article in *Challenge*.

[28] Unstable fiat money is, of course, not costless. See Milton Friedman, "The resource cost of irredeemable paper money," *Journal of Political Economy*, XCIV, June 1986, pp. 642-7.

[29] See James M. Buchanan, "Predictability: the criterion of monetary constitutions," ed. L.B. Yeager, *op. cit.*, and later "The Constitution of economic policy," in James M. Buchanan, *Economics: Between*

Predictive Science and Moral Philosophy eds. R.D. Tollison and V.J. Vanberg (College Station, Texas: Texas A and M University Press, 1987).

[30] Cukierman and Meltzer argue that an Authority, when it has information or thinks it has information superior to the community (as in the case of footnote 22 when it believed that more consumption temporarily was superior to higher steady state consumption) will result in the discretionary equilibrium whereas rules will preserve the optimum equilibrium but that in the event of full information there will not be this "cost of democratic government." Alex Cukierman and Allan H. Meltzer, "A positive theory of discretionary policy, the cost of democratic government and the benefits of a constitution." *Economic Inquiry*, XXIV, July 1986, pp. 367-89. Our argument is that in a world in which the final outcomes are unknown, we want an institutional form in which the fullest of political debate and discussion about the conduct of possibly discretionary monetary policy are encouraged. Indeed, one wants a forum in which the fullest possible explanation for the abandonment of rules governing the community takes place and that forum is political parties, government and Parliament, not an independent or quasi-independent Monetary Authority.

p 133:

COMMENTS ON
THOMAS K. RYMES' PAPER

Marc Lavoie, University of Ottawa

155 - 66

It is an honour for me to participate in this celebration of Professor Scott Gordon. In the seventies I was an undergraduate here at Carleton University, where I spent four very enjoyable years. I vaguely remember being told about the Coyne affair, and about the involvement of a professor of the department, when I took the introductory course in economics with Harvey Lithwick. I also remember sitting through one year of Honours seminars led by Tom Rymes, when some of the ideas he just presented today were probably percolating as he tried to convince us of the importance of Keynes' *General Theory* Chapter 17 and of Friedman's optimal theory of money.

The introductions made by both Peter Howitt and Tom Rymes should induce economists to become more modest and less arrogant about the worth of their trade. How can we have any confidence in our tools, our arguments, our principles, when as a group apparently following some kind of academic fashion, we can turn around 180 degrees in less than 30 years, radically changing our opinion and advice on such important matters as monetary policy? Keynes, to whom we all like to refer for some moral recomfort, once hoped that the economic profession would one day become as uncontroversial as dentistry. I am afraid rather that we have evolved towards the profession of dietitians, who in the days of Coyne, 30 years ago, favoured the consumption of margarine over that of butter, because the former was claimed to be healthy whereas the latter was said to be detrimental to our health. Today, they are claiming exactly the opposite.

Coming now to Tom Rymes' paper, I should say that it is a very neat synthesis and clear demonstration of the various neoclassical results and claims that have been put forward in the literature, recent or past, on efficient banking or optimal money growth rules. His unified treatment of some previously unrelated strands is a welcome addition. In particular, he demonstrates how some of those claims rely on the assumed stability of the model. For if there is instability of the sort he describes, then there is room for the mere existence of the central bank, for its discretionary behaviour, for fiat money or reserves not to be paid a market rate of interest, for Keynes's preference for liquidity. As a bonus, I might even add that Rymes almost convinces me that Keynes's infamous Chapter 17 and its previously incomprehensible own-rates of interest start to make sense.

To present his case against constitutional rules or the eradication of the Bank of Canada, Rymes has used precisely the same models, tools and assumptions as those who arrive at the opposite conclusions. This is a method which has gained widespread popularity nowadays. Keynesians will use rational expectations and the hypothesis of clearing markets, thus becoming new Keynesians, to derive results that contradict those of the new classicals; monetarists might use Keynesian assumptions (non-clearing markets) to derive classical results. This can be a very powerful methodology, as the past can testify, for instance when Tobin turned the tables on Friedman as the former managed to reproduce the latter's lags within a Keynesian framework.[1] But it also sometimes has some unforeseen consequences, for instance, when Samuelson attempted to defend neoclassical aggregate theory with a fixed-coefficient capital model.[2] Rymes has himself already taken advantage of this strategy, in his critique of the neoclassical measure of technical progress, where he tried to persuade mainstream economists that their measures were logically deficient even when assumptions most favourable to their case were being entertained.[3]

In the present instance, there is no doubt that any constitutional-rule zealot, once he has finished reading Tom Rymes' article or his future book, will find it difficult to keep arguing against some form of discretionary behaviour by the central bank. This fanatic may also be puzzled by the strange behaviour of a "managed" unstable economy. If I understand Rymes' story well enough, an attempt by the central bank to follow the optimal monetary behaviour, i.e., the attempt to raise the real rate of interest on reserves to the level of the marginal physical product of capital, will in the end bring decumulation and a lower permanent consumption per head. This is the reverse of what optimal behaviour would bring forth in the more standard stable case. To avoid being forced to abandon his faith, the zealot might then presume that the perverse results arrived at by Tom Rymes are due to some inappropriate assumption or to some incomplete specification. Expectations are usually the culprit. In the present case, the zealot could castigate the "unrealistic" assumption of increasing returns to scale on the services rendered by the real fiat money balances. He would invoke past surveys of evidence which demonstrate, for those searching long enough, that increasing returns to scale do not exist, and that diminishing returns are the rule. He would then use the first part of Rymes' paper, the part that deals with stable cases, to support his advocacy of constitutional rules.

What I am driving at is that the art of persuasion requires a two pronged approach. One must demonstrate that the theory under attack suffers from some internal inconsistency, or that its domain of validity is rather narrow, or even both. Then one must come up with an alternative. When one only draws an alternative, without a critique, there is the danger of being ignored, since those brought up in the dominating theory might not see why it should be abandoned. Those who lobby for that theory then have an open field in front of them. On the other hand, to attack a theory without proposing an alternative may not be viable either, since scientists abhor null sets. However, an alternative which is a variation on the dominating theory might not do. This is because, in the long run, the simple mainstream version will always reappear, under one guise or another. In my view, an alternative has to be a radical departure from the mainstream story. A successful alternative, one that lasts, will thus usually depart from the basis upon which the critique was initially conducted.[4]

Let me then come back to these standard optimal monetary growth models which, according to Rymes, are now being taken very seriously by a substantial portion of the money and banking economic profession, and which, as a consequence, must now be tackled head on by those who disagree with constitutional rules or the eradication of the central bank. Rymes has proceeded with an internal critique of optimal monetary theories, arguing that the scope of validity of their conclusions is limited to the stable cases, while assuming all of the other assumptions to hold. My critique will be more external. I shall look at the foundations of these models.

The monetary growth models of the kind described by Rymes have two basic characteristics: they have one sector, and two assets. There is a capital good and fiat money. One is never sure whether the word "capital" covers a real commodity or if it is only some kind of financial asset, but it is probably both. Fiat money, as pointed out on numerous occasions in the article, is artificially dropped out by helicopter. It must also occasionally be sucked off, presumably by some powerful flying vacuum.

First, I would like to take issue with the use of aggregate production functions. Doing this, I realize that I may sound like some sort of prehistoric beast, coming out of the mid-sixties to hunt down economists that are using all of those new and sophisticated techniques designed to properly apply the axiom of utility maximization. These same economists, on the production side, are usually putting forth a simple aggregate production function, with diminishing marginal products, where for instance employment is an inverse function of the real wage. They are then using all sorts of well-behaved substitution effects to demonstrate how optimally the market could drive the economy if only it could be left in the driver's seat. In the case of neoclassical monetary theory, diminishing returns with given capital or money stock are present, as are the proper substitution effects that induce the portfolio changes. The use of aggregate production functions is not innocuous. On that topic, I find an unexpected ally in David Laidler, whose position will not generate much sympathy from the new classicals. My understanding of Laidler is somewhat paradoxical. Any theoretical result obtained with aggregate production functions is doubtful, while empirical ones are worthless. Only critics of standard neoclassical models, Professor Rymes in this instance, should be allowed to make use of aggregate production functions. As Laidler states:

> The implication of (the Cambridge controversies) is that the aggregate production function had better be used in great care in macroeconomic analysis. If the object of the exercise is to demonstrate...the fragility of the "super-neutrality" of money, a growth model based on an aggregate production function may serve the purpose admirably. If super-neutrality breaks down easily (as it does) in so simple a theoretical case, it is unlikely to become suddenly robust in a more complicated environment. If indeed...the purpose is to investigate and theoretically explain the extent of departures from super-neutrality in any actual economy, such a model emphatically will not do.[5]

The Cambridge controversies have conclusively shown that long-period neoclassical theory is void. But the optimal money supply rule of Friedman, from which all the other recent neoclassical money and banking rules originate, is precisely of the long-period type.[6] All these neoclassical optimal monetary growth models are in the Wicksellian tradition, where capital requires a value measurement. They are not of the neo-Walrasian tradition, where quantities of capital only are needed. But in the case of long-period analysis, the Cambridge debate has taught us that prices are not scarcity indices, that substitution effects may be perverse, that higher mechanization ratios may be associated with lower permanent consumption per head or higher profit rates, that the marginal productivity of capital cannot be associated with the overall profit rate. The long-period analysis pursued by the partisans of optimum monetary policies, by Milton Friedman in particular, is precisely the type of analysis which is subject to the Cambridge/Sraffa capital critique. All optimal arrangements, based on the real rate of interest of money being equal to the marginal physical product of capital, or on the latter being equal to the natural growth rate plus the pure rate of time preference, just do not have any validity in a proper multi-sectoral long-period analysis. The fact that in an actual economy, the rates of profit or of real interest would approximate each other or the rate of time preference, gives us no indication of the efficiency of such an economy.

If neither Laidler nor myself are convincing enough, one might then be willing to consider further the logic of the money stock, rather than that of the capital stock. There are three points that I wish to make in this regard. First, I have always felt uncomfortable with the introduction of money balances in production functions. In what sense do money balances play a productive role, on a par with labour or machinery? How do money balances allow for increased production? And then, as in the typical neoclassical model depicted by Rymes, why does outside fiat money play that role while inside scriptural money does not? It is usually argued that the use of fiat money allows the economy not to waste part of its production into commodity money, so that less commodity capital is required for useful production, so to speak. But how do entrepreneurs make use of fiat money in their production process? This abstraction does not seem warranted.

There is a further problem, linked to the first I presume. The two assets, capital and fiat money, are supposed to be separate entities. This view arises, no doubt, from the North American banking system where reserves and cash are the liabilities of the central bank, to which correspond the government bonds which have been purchased in the past by the central bank. If the State were to spread fiat money all over North America, it could do so by forcing the central bank to purchase its bonds. But what if the State is building plants and machinery with those funds? Is fiat money still a separate entity from capital? A negative answer to this question is particularly striking in the case of European banking systems. The counterpart of fiat money there are the debts of the commercial banks vis-à-vis the central bank; and the counterpart of these banking debts are the outstanding loans remaining from past loans that banks awarded to firms for them to build up their capital stock.[7] This means that real money balances are part of the capital stock. The money balances m are integrated within the capital stock k. They are part of the same aggregate. They are not two distinct entities.

The problem here with neoclassical theory is that it has no theory of finance; it has no finance motive in the sense of Keynes' *Economic Journal* 1937 article. Firms decide to increase production. But where do the necessary financial resources come from? How are they created? Money and credit in neoclassical theory are not integrated within production, where they belong. In the words of Nicholas Kaldor and post-Keynesian authors, money is endogenous.[8] The creation of money is credit-driven, and credit is demand-determined. Loans make deposits, while outside money is a consequence rather than a cause of inside money. This means that the central bank can determine neither the stock of high-powered money nor the stock (or rate of growth) of money, although it can influence them through the rate of discount or the derived rates of interest.

In the typical neoclassical model, as described by Rymes for instance, the rate of inflation is a consequence of this dichotomy between the supply of money, forced upon households by the central bank, and the demand for money of households. The rate of inflation is the mechanism which equilibrates the demand for and the supply of money. The hypothesis of endogenous money creation cannot sustain such a mechanism. In a post-Keynesian system there cannot be excess money balances. Therefore neither inflation nor the price level can be explained by the supply of money. Furthermore, as I have pointed out above, the stock of capital and the stock of money cannot be considered independent of each other, nor can they be considered as distinct entities.[9] Finally, since money is credit-driven and demand-determined, constitutional rules forcing the central bank to set a certain rate of growth of money or high-powered money are *ultra vires*. "Constitutionalists" are missing the essential point: central banks cannot fix the money stock. They can only provide the financial system with an anchor, the rate of interest (or rate of discount), and observe how the demand for money responds to it. In the long run, after some tâtonnement, they may succeed on the average in reaching some target of money growth. But this target may be of little significance, due to the evolution of the velocity of money arising out of financial innovations. In the short run, when central banks do want to put a stop on things, they impose *credit* restrictions, nipping demand in the bud. Credit restrictions, however, are not popular with free-market advocates since they lack the anonymity of the money market.

After several years of toying with target growth rates of money aggregate, central bankers have finally recognized the importance and the relevance of these features of contemporary monetary economies. We are now being told that the Bank of Canada will eliminate the reserve requirements for chartered banks.[10] Despite this, the Bank will be able to control day-to-day interest rates, because chartered banks require balances at the Bank of Canada to settle payments within the Canadian clearing system. The abandonment of compulsory reserves is part of the deregulating and decompartmentalizing trends of financial services in Canada. One might say that with the suppression of reserves, i.e., non-interest bearing deposits, the Canadian financial system is coming closer to the optimal neoclassical state. One could also add that in so doing, the Bank of Canada is recognizing the endogenous nature of the money-creating process. Indeed, with the tightness of monetary policy soon to depend explicitly on the availability of settlement balances, the Canadian monetary system will be very similar to the European systems.[11]

Those economists who have relied on the excess reserves multiplier process to explain the creation of money deposits will now be hard-pressed to find a more suitable theory. In Europe, because reserves are not required in most monetary systems, there has always been widespread opposition to the standard view, with more attention devoted to the realism of the so-called transmission mechanism.

Rather than attempting to deal with this reality, neoclassical monetary growth economists prefer to describe a world where money is dropped off from helicopters, or eradicated through furnaces or vacuums, and where questions turn around whether helicopters should drop out the banknotes at random or aim towards those that already hold money balances. In such a world, we are being told that the central bank cannot influence the real rate of return of financial assets. The bureaucrats at the Bank of Canada have taken advantage of this, adopting a procedure to set the discount rate that reflects this belief. Rates of interest then appear to be mostly the result of market forces rather than of discretionary policy. Whenever interest rates are on the rise, we are told that market forces cannot be avoided, that U.S. rates have risen, that the Canadian dollar may depreciate, that the federal deficit is too large, or that inflation is rampant. But why are interest rates so high?

Since 1983, real rates of interest have on average been around 6%, while the rate of growth of productivity was about 1%. Those rentiers sitting on their fixed-return assets have thus benefited from a 5% surtax on the overall productive economy. This is quite extraordinary, considering that during the booming years of the postwar period, this rentier tax was generally negative, except in recessions. The present circumstances compared to the last 40 years are thus quite exceptional, since we face a combination of economic growth with a positive rentier tax on the productive economy. That the present accumulation with its decreasing purchasing power per Harrod person is only sustainable because of the unprecedented and huge federal government deficits, themselves partly induced by the high real interest rate, is an argument that seems to be lost to most observers.

Now, one might wish to discuss which constitutional rule of money supply growth, if any, should be imposed, or what kind of "adaptative monetary control," if any, should be put in place. But unless one assumes that the real rate of interest has at long last reached its proper (optimal) market level, or that the marginal physical product of capital, thanks to deregulation, has now reached new heights, as I was told by Michael Parkin two years ago, how can any economist be content with the present levels of interest rates? Why are real or nominal rates of interest so high? Why is there hardly any economist to question the wisdom of these high interest rates and that of the central banks?[12] Why are critiques of the policies of the Bank of Canada abandoned to provincial ministers, who have little credibility, or to organizations like The Committee on Monetary and Economic Reform, which perpetuates the *heretical* monetary tradition Keynes was talking about in the *General Theory*?[13] Do contemporary economists truly believe in the extent of the welfare losses they associate with inflation and non-optimal money policies? Is that why they do not disagree with the Governor's objective to eradicate inflation with appropriately high interest rates?

How is it possible to have a wider debate on the questions of monetary policy and interest rates? Rymes argues that the Bank of Canada should be brought towards a department of Monetary Affairs, so that the decisions of the central bank could be debated in the political arena, by those who were democratically elected to Parliament. The Minister of Monetary Affairs would have to field questions put to him about the behaviour of the monetary authorities. The elected minister, rather than a nominated governor, would have to take *effective* responsibility over monetary policy. As of now, the Minister of Finance puts the blame on the Governor, who in turn points the finger to external factors and market forces.

Before the recent electoral debates on free trade, I would certainly have agreed with Tom Rymes. Presumably, this is why he asked me to comment on his paper! It seems obvious that fiscal and monetary policies should be co-ordinated since they influence each other, and that politicians should get involved in the decision-making process of policies that have nation-wide repercussions.[14] It is obvious provided one does not believe in constitutional rules nor in optimal market-derived monetary rules. However, after the dreadful discussions on free trade that went on during the 1988 federal election campaign, I am not so sure anymore that politicians, with their propensity to draw on the lowest of the instincts of the voting public, should be allowed to deal with monetary matters. This negative assessment should perhaps be mollified. For Canada-U.S. free trade issues, like language issues, are not solely economically oriented: they are linked to nationalism and self-image, and as such are conducive to emotional displays. It should not be the case for monetary policy.

With the present institutional format, the efforts of the politicians have focused on the banking industry, rather than on interest rates. Politicians of all parties seem to have been mesmerized by the profits of the financial sector, and the fees which the banks have been charging for their services. What is ironic here is that the banks have started to behave the way economic theory recommends, paying interest on deposits and charging fees corresponding to the cost of the service being provided, while politicians are arguing on the grounds of fairness that new regulations and restrictions should be imposed on those service charges. No politician seems to realize that six percent rates of interest have much more damaging redistribution and employment consequences. But perhaps, with a department of Monetary Affairs, opposition M.P.s would come back to their senses, and criticize absurdly high interest rates rather than reasonable service charges.

In any case, pressure has been successfully exercised on the Bank of Canada some 30 years ago, after a crusade led by the person we are here to honour, Professor Scott Gordon. The institutional format today is the same, perhaps even slightly more favourable to a critique than it was then. What has changed is the academic climate among economists. Those who have not been convinced by the theoretical arguments that have become fashionable in academia should thus find some recomfort in the historical experience of 30 years ago. A good pamphlet could certainly put the Bank of Canada on the defensive and it should generate substantial media and political pressure on the central bank autocrats.[15] Such a pamphlet could certainly threaten the central bankers to have their ivory tower transformed into a department of Monetary Affairs subject, like all other departments, to the rules of Treasury Board and to those of parliamentary debates.

NOTES

[1] James Tobin, "Money and Income: Post Hoc Propter Hoc," *Quarterly Journal of Economics*, (May 1970), pp. 301-317.

[2] Paul Samuelson, "Parable and Realism in Capital Theory: The Surrogate Production Function," *Review of Economic Studies*, (June 1962), pp. 193-206.

[3] T.K. Rymes, *On Concepts of Capital and Technical Change*, (Cambridge University Press, Cambridge, 1971), ch. 3.

[4] All I am saying here is that I doubt that a successful Keynesian monetary theory can be built on neoclassical foundations. But this is only a point of view.

[5] David Laidler, "Notes for a Panel Discussion on the Relevance of the Work of the Stockholm School for Modern Economics," Stockholm, 1987, p. 2

[6] This is particularly well underlined by John Eatwell, "The Analytical Foundations of Monetarism," in J. Eatwell and M. Milgate (eds.), *Keynes's Economics and the Theory of Value and Distribution*, (Oxford University Press, Oxford, pp. 203-213. See also the revealing quote from Lucas, given by Rymes in his footnote 13.

[7] I have presented an introduction to these views in "Credit and Money: The Dynamic Circuit, Overdraft Economics, and Post-Keynesian Economics," in M. Jarsulic (ed.), *Money and Macro Policy*, (Kluwer-Nijhoff, Boston, 1985), pp. 63-85.

[8] See Nicholas Kaldor and James Trevithick, *A Keynesian Perspective on Money, Lloyds Bank Review*, (January 1981). pp. 1-19; see also Basil J. Moore's recent *Horizontalists and Verticalists: The Macroeconomics of Credit Money*, (Cambridge University Press, Cambridge, 1988.)

[9] In some neoclassical monetary growth models, however, the demand for money is proportional to the value of the capital stock (see Rudiger Dornbusch and Jacob A. Frenkel, "Inflation and Growth," *Journal of Credit, Money and Banking*, (February 1973), pp. 141-156.

[10] See John W. Crow, "The Work of Canadian Monetary Policy," *Bank of Canada Review*, (February 1988), p. 7.

[11] Indeed in one of the two cases considered, the participants at the

clearinghouse would be continuously indebted to the Bank of Canada, and the lending rate would be a function of the amounts borrowed by each chartered bank on other direct clearers. In both of the cases described, the control of the money stock is very indirect, through the pressure of interest rates. See Bank of Canada, "Discussion Paper on the Implementation of Monetary Policy in the Absence of Reserve Requirements," (September 29, 1987).

[12] Peter Howitt for instance, in the last footnote to his paper, tells us that the monetary policy he is suggesting is precisely of the kind being pursued by the present Governor of the Bank of Canada.

[13] COMER: Committee on Monetary and Economic Reform, with economists and businessmen from both sides of the border.

[14] Those who worry that politicians will do to monetary policy what they have already done to fiscal policy, should read the arguments put forth by William Greider to the effect that a non-independent control bank will force politicians to be more responsible ("The Money Question," *World Policy Journal*, Vol. 5, (Fall 1988), p. 592).

[15] In the late seventies, a booklet by A. Donner and D. Peters (*The Monetarist Counter-Revolution: A Critique of Canadian Monetary Policy*, James Lorimer, Toronto. 1979) generated media attention and forced the Bank of Canada to respond, although the critique was not particularly innovative.

Chapter VII

DINNER REMARKS

Paul Fox, University of Toronto

Ted English, Carleton University

Larry Read, Carleton University

PAUL FOX

Mr. Chairman, I am honoured to be asked to say a few words tonight on this auspicious occasion honouring Scott Gordon.

I first met Scott Gordon when we both came to Carleton as new, young faculty members exactly 40 years ago.

I was impressed by him immediately, Not only was he outgoing, warm, and genial, but he was also very bright and shrewd. How shrewd I discovered later when I learned that he had managed to negotiate a salary that was five hundred dollars a year more than mine. Since my salary was $3,000 a year, there was a considerable percentage differential. In addition, he also had secured an appointment as an assistant professor in economics while I was a humble lecturer in political science.

Now, since I am in the company of economists tonight rather than political scientists, the majority of you may well believe that those differentials in salary and status were sensible and quite appropriate to the two disciplines. However, I immediately perceived the reality, which was that H. Scott Gordon was a very smart young man who was destined to go places. That perception has been proven true, obviously, since we are all here tonight to celebrate Scott's distinguished career and accomplishments.

Scott made his mark at Carleton as soon as he arrived. The cynics among you may say that that wasn't too difficult since the College was so small in 1948. It was small. As I recall, Carleton then had about 25 full-time faculty members and something like 400 full-time students. It also was still a college, not yet a university, and it was located in a modest building at the corner of First Avenue and Lyon in what I must remember to call the "former" ladies' college rather than the "old" ladies' college. We were all crammed into one building since the library extension was yet to come.

But though it was modest, Carleton had a number of very able faculty members and rising stars. Munro Beattie, David Farr, Frank MacKinnon, James Gibson, Bert Nesbitt, and Wilfrid Eggleston were already there, and we were soon joined by Don Rowat, John Porter, Ted English and other promising young scholars.

Scott became one of the intellectual leaders at once. He delivered excellent lectures which attracted a growing number of students and he engaged in serious scholarship. He was well-read, thoughtful, judicious, opinionated, and provocative. (With those qualities, it is no wonder he turned out to be a distinguished economist.)

He was an ideal colleague because he was both a stimulus and a support. We — and by that I mean the small group of social scientists — talked and argued a great deal, and Scott was always in the thick of things, adding to the discussion, pushing the debate on, and thinking through to a conclusion with great lucidity. In the process, he educated the rest of us.

I remember, for instance, raising with him casually one day an obscure point about rent which I had found in some writings by the British Fabians. Scott immediately picked it up, related it to his own knowledge, embellished it, and worked through to a conclusion. He said, "You know, this is an interesting and important point. We should write an article about it." And in due course, after a good deal more labour by both of us, a joint article was published in the *Canadian Journal of Economics and Political Science.*

But Scott's interests were not confined to the ivory tower. He was very interested also in public affairs He never seemed to be without a copy of the latest federal budget, or White Paper or financial or economic statement nor indeed without opinions about it. Usually those opinions were more negative than positive. At that point in history the Liberal Party had been in power in Ottawa for what seemed to be an eternity — 15 years going on 20 — and Scott appeared to be dedicated to getting them out of power before they died of old age.

These were salad days, when we were young, energetic, confident, and joyful. A new world was arising out of the muck and mire of the

Second World War, Canada was entering a prolonged economic boom, and our minds and hearts were racing. We worked with zest, and we played with gusto. Believe it or not, Scott and some of the rest of us even took up swimming regularly in the Chateau Laurier pool.

We also savoured the political scene in Ottawa. Scott had a tiny Austin coupe and one day during a federal by-election in Carleton constituency three or four of us jammed into Scott's tiny, ancient vehicle and proceeded to a famous "contradictory meeting" at which the rival candidates met and debated in front of their electors. It was that period's version of the current television debates. This meeting was held in a tiny church hall in Richmond, outside Ottawa, and the two major contestants were George Drew, the new federal Progressive Conservative leader and former Premier of Ontario, and Eugene Forsey, who was then running as a CCF candidate. Forsey's nominator was Bill Temple, a fanatical temperance advocate. He assailed Drew as an evil monster who had introduced cocktail bars in Ontario which had led to the debauchery of hundreds of innocent young girls in hotel rooms. Drew threatened to punch Temple in the nose, and Forsey assured the assembled voters that he (Eugene Forsey) and his family had been temperance for four generations. Whereupon a hard-boiled farmer standing next to Scott and me cried out, "And the more fool you!"

In addition to his teaching, his scholarship, his interest in public affairs, and his genius for friendship, Scott made another significant contribution to Carleton which greatly affected its future. Since you may not be aware of it and it is important, I would like to draw it to your attention before concluding.

When Scott and I arrived at Carleton in 1948, the College was in the throes of finding its identity and destiny. The College, as you probably know, had originated as a wartime expedient to provide some sort of adult education courses for the swollen tide of military and civilian personnel who had flooded into the national capital during the war. Although Henry Marshall Tory had been active in the establishment of Carleton and he had already founded two Canadian universities, few thought that the College was a nascent university. It seemed destined to go on being a community centre, or at best an Ottawa version of Sir George Williams College which had been founded by the YMCA in Montreal for after-hours, part-time students.

However, as aspiring young scholars of Scott's calibre were appointed to the faculty in growing numbers, the direction of the College began to change. We could see an opportunity to build a university of quality in Ottawa. The struggle was not easy. The elements in the College who preferred the adult education style clung to their conception tenaciously while the New Jerusalem visionaries fought for changes.

Scott was in the forefront of the battle to achieve university ideals. In curriculum committees, in examiners' meetings, and in faculty and council debates on admission standards, grading rules, promotion policies, and all the other myriad ways in which an institution by its decisions identifies itself as a university, Scott fought a valiant battle, steadfastly, patiently, courteously, but remorselessly, never deviating from his conception of what a good university must be.

As one who took part in the struggle, I must say that it was trying, troublesome, and exhausting. But I think it was successful. If Carleton University today is a recognized place of higher learning, then it is because Scott Gordon, in no small way, was here and contributed his great talents not just to excellent teaching, fine scholarship, and productive collegiality, but to the building of a university worthy of that name.

Long may Scott continue to thrive and exert his beneficent influence!

TED ENGLISH

One of my greatest regrets is that I have seen so little of Barbara and Scott in recent years. I missed the celebration a few years ago at Queen's. We had left a few weeks before on a sabbatical leave overseas.

I remember quite clearly the day in the fall of 1949 when I was welcomed to Carleton by the Gordons, at dinner at their home on Delaware Street. From the outset Scott showed that warmth and hospitality combined with clear-headed, even-tempered reason which we always associate with him. I was a rather insecure, nervous young teacher that first year or so. Perhaps my memory has become mercifully weak, but I do not recall a word of impatience or direct criticism. I do recall many occasions when Scott provided encouragement and unintrusive advice.

One such occasion was that of my first journal article — a review article of a study on the electrical appliance industry, prepared by three well-known economists — Frank Knox and David Slater, then both at Queen's, and Clarence Barber. They seemed to me to support or tolerate protection on the grounds that in the early 1950s the industry was vulnerable to U.S. competition. I suggested that the protection was a support of inefficiency and not therefore an appropriate remedy. My language was direct but not really so much so as the title which the journal attached to the article without my permission, "Canadian Electrical Industry Confuses Economists." For a young economist seeking to convince his professional colleagues, I was embarrassed, but Scott was tougher stock and was reassuring. When one of the authors complained to Scott, I was later told that he defended me on the grounds of the validity of my case. However, another of the authors, David Slater, not long afterwards invited me to work with him on two Gordon Commission studies in 1956.

In the 1950s, it was a little department, only three of us, Scott, Tom Brewis and myself, joined later by Steve Kaliski. A major feature of Scott's leadership was in two very significant areas, as a teacher, and as a scholar. I recall no student or fellow faculty commenting critically on Scott as a teacher; I heard many positive opinions. As for scholarship, Scott's was broadly based. Although he is mainly known as a specialist in monetary economics (money and banking) and history of economic thought, he had made a very important contribution in the 1950s to resource theory with his articles on common property resources, which ranked with Tony Scott's work as cornerstones of Canadian contributions in this area.

The building years (baby boom years) saw the Department grow from four persons in 1962 to 16 in 1966. In 1962 I went on leave to Montreal for four years at the Private Planning Association of Canada, precursor of the C.D. Howe Institute. I want to make it clear that before I left I was responsible for adding Tom Rymes to the Department. I don't want Scott to be credited or blamed for that. But in the next few years, Scott brought in Irwin Gillespie, Harvey Lithwick and Gilles Paquet.

Certainly the most memorable event of that first decade was the Coyne affair. After 1957, the resource boom of the decade petered out. Private investment lapsed, and unemployment increased. But price increases also occurred. Not a real inflation, but a modest dose of stagflation, fuelled by weaker demand and excess capacity in primary export sectors, and more public investment in public goods, highways, etc., reflected in income generated without parallel increases in consumer goods productivity. Mr. Coyne attacked the inflation with a tight monetary policy, raising interest rates, drawing in foreign capital, mainly to finance public capital, but raising the value of the Canadian dollar and thereby increasing imports and further decreasing exports. But the capital inflow was dominant, keeping the dollar higher than was justified in the real economic circumstances of the day. (A brief aside; I noted with interest in this afternoon's papers, especially that of Professor Howitt, that monetary economists are now using later theoretical developments to reinterpret the events of 1960 in the light of 1980s macroeconomic theory. This surely reflects the basic error of monetary economists that whatever the burden on the real economy, it must be borne in the interest of intellectual coherence in their field). The real criticism of Coyne, so far as I was concerned, was that a policy that kept exchange rates up and induced provincial government debt-financing to rely on U.S. sources was making it difficult to achieve the needed rationalization of Canadian industry. Unilateral tariff reduction would have been a better choice because it would have encouraged improvement in efficiency without handicapping exports.

Scott and Larry Read fired the first salvo in their criticism of the selection of the use of statistics by the bank. Later came the famous meeting in the fall of 1960 when, at a McGill Conference on an entirely different subject, Harry Eastman, Stefan Stykolt and Scott Gordon conceived the idea of a letter to the Minister of Finance, calling for government intervention to counter the Governor's amazing policy. Many people are not aware that the intention was to keep the economists' advice to the Minister private. Of course, that was naïve, especially since the letter was circulated for signatures to many university departments of economics. The letter's essence was leaked to the press; we believe in Montreal, probably from McGill. In any case, I recall the late afternoon when we were called by Bruce MacDonald of the Globe and Mail. After consultation with Scott, we decided to release it and I actually read it over the phone to Bruce. It was published the next day, or the day after. It was on the same day that, as it happened, the Board of Governors was meeting to consider questions of academic tenure. It was usually under the chairmanship of James Coyne, though I do not know for sure if he was at that meeting. A nice touch of irony. There is no evidence that either the Governor or President Dunton ever indicated to the Carleton faculty members who signed the notorious letter that we had embarrassed him or the University. But then, Dunton was a man who understood academic freedom, and the wisdom of moderate if any reaction in such circumstances.

The event contributed in an important way to a rise in public profile of academic economists in the early 1960s, much more activity in submissions to Royal Commissions, and appearances before parliamentary committees, participation on party policy conferences also became more common, e.g. the Liberal Conference in Kingston in 1960 and the Conservative one in Fredericton in 1964.

But, as Scott can attest, not all those in the political and bureaucratic establishment received criticism kindly, and as one of the main authors of the Coyne criticism, Scott experienced some of the consequences of a society not yet mature enough to receive serious public policy debate on its merits. I thought I could detect a retreat into history of doctrine at the time, to the immense good fortune of that field. However, he would, I am sure, be likely to admit that the longer term issues in the development of his science in the context of its times was his first and lasting love, next of course to Barbara.

And so he left us, but not before setting us on a course that continues to give some place to public policy debates as well as theory and applied methodology. Well, we are still at it — including free trade and all that. Fortunately, at least until next Tuesday (election day, November 1988), it will be easier for professionals from the U.S. to gain temporary entry to Canada to supply services to Canadians. Others could benefit from your wisdom and well-controlled emotions.

174 Pinner Remarks *Welfare, Property Rights and Economic Policy*

LARRY READ

Among friends it is possible to speak discreetly about affairs. I want to talk about how I got innocently involved in the beginning of an affair. Those of us who knew Scott Gordon in "the good old days" came to realize that he was carrying on a protracted and passionate affair with the Bank of Canada. It was a love/hate affair: no doubt the Freudians would say that Scott had a deeply suppressed desire to be Governor of the Bank.

My involvement at the beginning of this affair was completely innocent. One day near the middle of the academic year 1957-58 Scott and I found ourselves arguing the ramifications of the following hypothetical case: (1) A branch banking system with one of the banks carrying a significant slice of the nation's banking business — let us say Bank A does 20 percent of the business. (2) The banks keep a cash reserve equal to 10 percent of deposit liabilities (as the Canadian banks did at that time). And (3) the central bank freely makes loans to the banks at the bank rate. Under these conditions Bank A could borrow a million dollars from the central bank, the banking system could parley this into a ten million increase in loans and deposits, and Bank A's portion of this would be two million. Thus Bank A could easily increase the money supply by its borrowing activity and profit nicely from it unless the bank rate rose to *double* the commercial loan interest rate. We were rather excited by this possibility. However, on further reflection we realized that the central bank could offset any attempt of Bank A to increase the money supply by selling a million dollars of securities in the open market with every million dollars it loaned to Bank A.

We thought the discussion of this case an interesting one, wrote it up and booked it as a paper for the Canadian Political Science Association meetings in Edmonton in June 1958.

Some weeks before the June meetings Scott picked up the rumour that the Bank of Canada's annual report was out and hurried downtown to pick up an early copy. Scott and I examined the report together and were surprised to find that without notice to its readers the Bank had changed its definition of the money supply: federal government deposits with the chartered banks, formerly excluded, were now included as part of the money supply. We asked ourselves the question, Why?, and settled down to comb the report for an answer.

We found that the money supply was not only defined in a new way but calculated in a new way, i.e. on a month-end basis rather than as formerly on an average of Wednesdays basis. Monthly variations in the money supply as newly defined and calculated supported the proposition that the Bank of Canada had promoted an expansion of the money supply for some months; the monthly variations in the money supply as hitherto defined and calculated did not. The Bank had been strongly criticized for its tight money policy at this time. Now by the devices of a volatile definition and method of measurement the Bank had extricated itself from sharp criticism. Moreover, we discovered that the Bank had concocted these devices some time in the midst of preparing the report: some statements still remained which clearly presupposed the previously standard definition and calculation of the money supply.

Scott and I were *outraged* — or, in other words, were *delighted.* It is not often that the academic watchdogs of public morals catch senior public officials *in flagrante.*

A paper on the matter was inevitable. We agreed that a consistent style throughout would be more effective; and since I knew that Scott's mastery of polemics was far superior to my own I suggested that he write the paper. In fact I suggested that he fly this one solo. However, since we had done the investigating as a team, Scott wanted the paper to be a joint one. We approached the Canadian Political Science Association and they agreed that we could substitute this new tract for our previously accepted paper.

Amusingly, this turned out to be a life-saver for us for another reason: shortly afterwards, in perusing Keynes' *Treatise on Money,* Scott found the argument of our previous paper neatly set forth in an extended footnote.

So Scott dashed off the paper and we did some final polishing on our way out to Edmonton together by train. In giving the paper its title we had to overcome some obvious temptations, such as "The Other Side of the Coyne" but we settled for the more serious "The Political Economics of the Bank of Canada."

In Edmonton we were received by a large and appreciative audience and Scott read the paper in appropriately grave tones. The Bank of Canada was ably defended by Bill Lawson (later Deputy Governor of the Bank). He drew from us the confession that whereas Scott had typically used the Bank's old definition of money supply, I had for some time been using the Bank's new definition. "So there you have it!" Bill said. We replied that neither of us thought it appropriate to alter our definition without notice to bolster our case in the middle of an argument.

As I recall my main contribution to the debate was to suggest in an excess of youthful exuberance and arrogance that we should commend Bill Lawson for his unswerving loyalty to a governor who displayed such versatility in defining the money supply. Before the day was out Bill happily balanced the score by saying, "And as for Read, where is he now? In the Department of Religion? Clearly where he belongs! Clearly where he belongs!"

Meanwhile, "back at the ranch" the local Ottawa papers were giving the affair suitable publicity. The Ottawa Journal's page one headline read: "Carleton Professors Charge Bank's Reports Misleading." Most impressive was the account, I think in the Citizen, of a senior Bank official who, when confronted by reporters with what we had said, responded "Wow!" Many years later Joe Scanlon of the School of Journalism told me somewhat more prosaically that he thought the paper was one of the best pieces of investigative journalism ever done in Canada.

My account ends here. Some years later when the Scott Gordon/Bank of Canada affair had expanded into "the economists versus the Bank of Canada," I thought it high time that I take Bill Lawson's advice: I fled to the tower and barricaded myself in the Department of Religion. That unfortunately had the negative effect of ending what might otherwise have been a most profitable long-term liaison of Scott Gordon with theology.

PUBLICATIONS OF H. SCOTT GORDON

1950: "The Pragmatic Basis of Economic Theory," *Canadian Journal of Economics and Political Science.*

1951: "The Early Fabians, Economists and Reformers," (with P.W. Fox). *Canadian Journal of Economics and Political Science.*

"The Trawler Question in the United Kingdom and Canada," *Dalhousie Review.*

1952: "On a Misinterpretation of the Law of Diminishing Returns in Marshall's *Principles,*" *Canadian Journal of Economics and Political Science.*

"Government Price Support Policy," *The Business Quarterly.*

1953: "An Economic Approach to the Optimum Utilization of Fishery Resources," *Journal of Fisheries Research Board of Canada.*

1954: "The Meaning of Social Security," *The Business Quarterly.*

"The Economic Theory of a Common Property Resource: The Fishery," *Journal of Political Economy.*

1955: "Economic Factors in Catch Fluctuations," *Journal of the Fisheries Research Board of Canada.*

"The London *Economist* and the High Tide of Laissez-Faire," *Journal of Political Economy.*

1957: "Obstacles to Agreement and Control in the Fishing Industry," in R. Turvey and J. Wiseman (eds.), *The Economics of Fisheries*, Food and Agriculture Organization of the U.N.

1958: "Economics and the Conservation Question," *The Journal of Law and Economics.*

"The Political Economics of the Bank of Canada," (with L.M. Read) *Canadian Journal of Economics and Political Science.*

1960:   "Darwinism and Social Thought," in H.H.J. Nesbitt, (ed.) *Darwin in Retrospect*, Ryerson Press, Toronto.

1961:   *The Economists Versus the Bank of Canada*, Ryerson Press, Toronto.

"The Bank of Canada in a System of Responsible Government," *Canadian Journal of Economics and Political Science.*

"Planning for Economic Progress — Natural Resources and Capital Investment," in M. Oliver (ed.) *Social Purpose for Canada*, University of Toronto Press.

"The Historical Perspective: Nineteenth Century Trade Theory and Policy," in H.E. English (ed.) *Canada and the New International Economy*, University of Toronto Press.

1963:   "Ideas of Economic Justice," *Daedalus.*

1965:   *Canada: An Appraisal of its Needs and Resources* (with George W. Wilson and Stanislaw Judek) 20th Century Fund, and University of Toronto Press.

1966:   *An Assessment of the Role of the Economic Council of Canada and an Appraisal of its Second Annual Review*, Canadian Trade Committee of the Private Planning Association of Canada, Montreal.

"A Twenty-Year Perspective: Some Reflections on the Keynesian Revolution in Canada," Canadian Trade Committee, *Canadian Economic Policy Since the War*, Montreal.

1967:   "Das Kapital: A Centenary Appreciation — Discussion," *American Economic Review, Proceedings.*

1968:   "Walter Bagehot: Economic Contributions," *International Encyclopedia of the Social Sciences*, Macmillan Co. and the Free Press.

"Laissez-Faire," *International Encyclopedia of the Social Sciences.*

"Why Does Marxian Exploitation Theory Require a Labor Theory of Value?" *Journal of Political Economy.*

The Close of the Galbraithian System," *Journal of Political Economy.*

1969:   "Mill, Population, and Liberty," *The Mill News Letter.*

"The Galbraithian System — Rejoinder," *Journal of Political Economy.*

1970:   "On Rereading Marx's Capital," in G.W. Wilson, F. Gehrels, and H.M. Oliver, (eds.) *Essays in Economic Analysis and Policy*, Indiana University Press.

Social Science and Modern Man (Plaunt Lectures at Carleton University) University of Toronto Press.

1971: "The Ideology of Laissez-Faire," in A.W. Coats (ed.) *The Classical Economists and Economic Policy*, London: Methuen

1972: *Social Institutions, Change, and Progress*, (Woodward Lectures in Economics), Vancouver, University of British Columbia Press.

"The Quality of Pleasure: Mill and Edgeworth," *The Mill News Letter*.

"Two Monetary Inquiries in Great Britain: The Macmillan Committee of 1931 and the Radcliffe Committee of 1959," *Journal of Money, Credit and Banking*.

1973: "Alfred Marshall and the Development of Economics as a Science," Ronald N. Giere and Richard S. Westfall (eds.) *Foundations of Scientific Method: The Nineteenth Century*, Bloomington, Indiana University Press.

"The Wage-Fund Controversy: The Second Round," *Journal of Philosophy*.

"John Rawls' Difference Principle, Utilitarianism, and the Optimum Degree of Inequality," *Journal of Philosophy*.

"Today's Apocalypses and Yesterday's," *American Economic Review, Proceedings*.

1974: "Frank Knight and the Tradition of Liberalism," *Journal of Political Economy*.

1975: "The Quality Problem in Utilitarianism," *The Mill News Letter*.

"The Political Economy of Big Questions, and Small Ones," *Canadian Public Policy*.

"The Eisenhower Administration: The Doctrine of Shared Responsibility," in Craufurd D. Goodwin (ed.) *Exhortation and Controls: The Search for a Wage-Price Policy*, 1945-1971. Washington, D.C., The Brookings Institution.

1976: "The Basic Analytical Structure of Malthusian Theory," in T.R. Malthus, *An Essay on the Principle of Population* (ed. by Philip Appleman), N.Y., Norton.

"The New Contractarians," *Journal of Political Economy*.

1977: *The Demand and Supply of Government: What We Want and*

What We Get. Economic Council of Canada, Discussion Paper no. 79.

"Social Science and Value Judgments," *Canadian Journal of Economics* (Presidential Address to Canadian Economics Association).

1978:   "Should Economists Pay Attention to Philosophers?" *Journal of Political Economy.*

1979:   "A Critique of Sociobiology," Discussion Paper No. 346, Queen's University, Institute for Economic Research.

1980:   *Welfare, Justice and Freedom*, Columbia University Press.

"Emmanuel's Extension of Marxian Transformation Theory," (with N. Spulber) Discussion Paper 80-6, Department of Economics, Indiana University.

"Sociobiology," *Transactions of the Royal Society of Canada.*

1981:   "The Nature of Economics: Some Notes on the Dismal Science," D.C. Smith (ed.) *Economic Policy Advising in Canada*, Montreal: C.D. Howe Institute.

"The Political Economy of F.A. Hayek," *Canadian Journal of Economics.*

1982:   "A Paraphrase Version of Keynes' *General Theory*," Discussion Paper No. 476, Queen's University, Institute for Economic Research.

"Why Did Marshall Transpose the Axes?" *Eastern Economic Journal.*

1984:   "Citation Classic," (Paper listed above 1954: *Journal of Political Economy*) *Current Contents, Social and Behavioral Sciences*, January 23.

Bienestar, Justicia y Libertad. Buenos Aires: Abeledo-Perrot. (Spanish translation of *Welfare, Justice and Freedom* (1980).

1985:   "The Market as Commons: Is Catching Customers Like Catching Fish?" (with Klaus Stegemann) *De Economist.*

1986:   "Some Mild Criticisms of Some Modest Proposals," Karl Brunner (ed.), *Economics, Theology, and the Social Order.* University of Rochester Center for Research in Government Policy and Business.

"Deutsch's *Distributive Justice*: A Review Essay," Warren Samuels (ed.) *Research in the History of Economic Thought and Methodology*, Vol. 4.

1988: "The Venetian Republic in the History and Theory of Constitutionalism," Conference Group on Italian Politics and Society, *Newsletter* No. 25.

1989: "Why Does *Homo sapiens* Differ?" *Journal of Social and Biological Structures.*

"Darwin and Political Economy: The Connection Reconsidered," *Journal of the History of Biology.*

1990: "How Many Kinds of Things are there in the World?" Distinguished Faculty Research Lecture, Indiana University

In progress:

The History and Philosophy of Social Science. To be published by Routledge in 1991.

"The Economics Profession: Changes and Problems," To be published in H.C. Rechtenwald, ed., *Die Zukunft der Öconomischen Wissenschaft.*

A book dealing with the social thought of Alfred Russel Wallace.